Simon Wiesenthal

These and other titles are included in The Importance Of biography series:

THE IMPORTANCE OF

Simon Wiesenthal

by Linda Jacobs Altman

Lucent Books, P.O. Box 289011, San Diego, CA 92198-9011

Library of Congress Cataloging-in-Publication Data

Altman, Linda Jacobs, 1943–
     The importance of Simon Wiesenthal / by Linda Jacobs
Altman.
          p.   cm.—(The importance of)
     Includes bibliographical references and index.
     Summary: Examines the life and accomplishments of
Holocaust survivor Simon Wiesenthal, whose passion for justice has brought many Nazis to account for their horrific
deeds.
     ISBN 1-56006-490-0 (lib. bdg. : alk. paper)
     1. Wiesenthal, Simon—Juvenile literature. 2. Jews—Aus-
tria—Vienna—Biography—Juvenile literature.   3. Holocaust,
Jewish (1939–1945)—Biography—Juvenile literature.   4. Nazi
hunters—Biography—Juvenile literature. 5. War criminals—
Germany—Juvenile literature. 6. Holocaust survivors—Biography—Juvenile literature. [1. Wiesenthal, Simon. 2. Holocaust
survivors. 3. War criminals—Germany. 4. Holocaust, Jewish
(1939–1945)] I. Title.   III. Series.
DS135.A93W5318   2000
940.53'18'092—dc21   99–36808
[B]   CIP

Copyright 2000 by Lucent Books, Inc., P.O. Box 289011,
San Diego, California 92198-9011

Printed in the U.S.A.

Contents

Foreword

THE IMPORTANCE OF biography series deals with individuals who have made a unique contribution to history. The editors of the series have deliberately chosen to cast a wide net and include people from all fields of endeavor. Individuals from politics, music, art, literature, philosophy, science, sports, and religion are all represented. In addition, the editors did not restrict the series to individuals whose accomplishments have helped change the course of history. Of necessity, this criterion would have eliminated many whose contribution was great, though limited. Charles Darwin, for example, was responsible for radically altering the scientific view of the natural history of the world. His achievements continue to impact the study of science today. Others, such as Chief Joseph of the Nez Percé, played a pivotal role in the history of their own people. While Joseph's influence does not extend much beyond the Nez Percé, his nonviolent resistance to white expansion and his continuing role in protecting his tribe and his homeland remain an inspiration to all.

These biographies are more than factual chronicles. Each volume attempts to emphasize an individual's contributions both in his or her own time and for posterity. For example, the voyages of Christopher Columbus opened the way to European colonization of the New World. Unquestionably, his encounter with the New World brought monumental changes to both Europe and the Americas in his day. Today, however, the broader impact of Columbus's voyages is being critically scrutinized. *Christopher Columbus,* as well as every biography in The Importance Of series, includes and evaluates the most recent scholarship available on each subject.

Each author includes a wide variety of primary and secondary source quotations to document and substantiate his or her work. All quotes are footnoted to show readers exactly how and where biographers derive their information, as well as provide stepping stones to further research. These quotations enliven the text by giving readers eyewitness views of the life and times of each individual covered in The Importance Of series.

Finally, each volume is enhanced by photographs, bibliographies, chronologies, and comprehensive indexes. For both the casual reader and the student engaged in research, The Importance Of biographies will be a fascinating adventure into the lives of people who have helped shape humanity's past and present, and who will continue to shape its future.

IMPORTANT DATES IN THE LIFE OF SIMON WIESENTHAL

1908
Wiesenthal born in Buczacz on December 30.

1926
Rosa Wiesenthal, Simon's mother, remarries.

1939
Nazi Germany invades Czechoslovakia. Hitler signs non-aggression pact with Stalin. Nazi Germany invades Poland; WWII begins.

1938
Nazi Germany annexes Austria.

1943
Cyla Wiesenthal smuggled out of camp and into hiding. In April, Simon is selected for death then saved by Kohlrautz.

1910 **1920** **1930** **1935** **1940**

1915
Father is killed in WWI; the family moves to Vienna.

1923
Simon meets future wife in school. His brother Hillel dies.

1932
Simon goes to Prague to study architecture.

1936
He marries Cyla Müller on September 9.

1941
German troops invade Soviet-occupied Poland, then take Lvov. Wiesenthal is arrested; Simon and Cyla sent to Janowska labor camp.

1942
Wisenthal's mother is deported to Belzec extermination camp.

1945
American troops liberate Mauthausen concentration camp on May 5. In December, Simon and Cyla Wiesenthal are reunited.

1985
Wiesenthal takes up the cause of Gypsy Holocaust victims.

1967
He publishes his first autobiography, *The Murderers Among Us.*

1977
Simon Wiesenthal Center is founded in Los Angeles.

1954
Wiesenthal begins closing the Linz Documentation Center.

1986
He is passed over for the Nobel Peace Prize.

1945	1960	1970	1980	1990	2000

1946
Paulinka Wiesenthal, their daughter, is born.

1989
He publishes his second autobiography, *Justice Not Vengeance.*

1997
He publishes a new version of *The Sunflower.*

1961
He moves to Vienna; establishes new Documentation Center.

1970
The first version of *The Sunflower* is published.

Speaker for the Dead

After World War II ended in 1945, a stunned world confronted the horror that would become known as the Holocaust. In their quest to build a "master race," Nazi Germany had wiped out whole classes of "inferior" people. They killed Gypsies, homosexuals, Poles, and Russians, but mostly they killed Jews. Six million men, women, and children died simply because of their Jewish origins.

When Allied troops liberated death camps—Chelmo, Bergen-Belsen, Birkenau, and Majdanek—they saw unimaginable sights. They saw gas chambers for killing people and ovens for burning the bodies. They saw "hospitals" where doctors had performed inhuman experiments and barracks where living skeletons quietly starved. They saw pits filled with quicklime and corpses. Everywhere there was the stench of death.

SIMON WIESENTHAL: SURVIVOR

Simon Wiesenthal knows that death-smell all too well. He spent the war years in more

Concentration camp ovens were used by the Nazis to incinerate Jewish corpses.

A Short Vocabulary of the Holocaust

anti-Semitism: Hatred of Jews as a group.

Aryan: Word used by the Nazis to describe people of German and Northern European ancestry.

concentration camp: a prison camp where Nazis used Jews and others as slave labor.

extermination camps: prison camps built to accommodate mass killing on a routine basis

führer: Leader. Term used for Adolf Hitler.

Final Solution: Nazi code name for the complete extermination of European Jewry.

genocide: The systematic killing of an entire group.

ghetto: A run-down neighborhood where all Jews in an area were forced to live.

holocaust: (small "h") Wholesale destruction and loss of life; a sacrifice that is consumed by fire; burnt offering.

Holocaust: the systematic killing of six million European Jews.

Jewish question/problem: Nazi term for the impact of Jews on European culture.

master race: refers to the idea that Germans were superior to other peoples and therefore entitled to rule.

Nazi: first letters (in German) of the National Socialist German Workers Party. A racist dictatorship that ruled Germany from 1933-1945.

selection: The process of review, whereby Nazi officials decided who was to live and who was to die.

SS—*Shutzstaffel* ("protection squad"): A secret police unit that began as Adolf Hitler's personal bodyguard. They later became responsible for dealing with the Jews.

subhumans: Refers to Jews, Gypsies, Poles, Russians, and others whom the Nazis considered inferior.

Third Reich: Third empire; Nazi term for their dictatorship.

than half a dozen different camps. Several times he stood on the brink of death. Each time, some strange twist of fate pulled himback. When American troops liberated the Mauthausen camp on May 5, 1945, Wiesenthal was there; an emaciated shadow of a man with haunted eyes.

His life would never go back to what it had been before the Holocaust. With all he had seen and suffered, he could not let that happen. "Since my liberation, there is not one day that I have forgotten that I am a survivor,"[1] he once said.

Camp survivor Simon Wiesenthal.

In biographies of Wiesenthal, information about his childhood and pre-Holocaust life is sketchy. He rarely talks or writes about that time. He wrote in his book, *Justice Not Vengeance:*

> My private life is uninteresting. I am married, I have a daughter, I have grandchildren—they mean everything to me, but they are of no interest to the general public. Of interest alone is my life in relation to Nazism: I have survived the Holocaust and I have tried to preserve the memory of the dead. . . . It is solely. . . as a witness, that I write now.[2]

WIESENTHAL'S MISSION

Simon Wiesenthal tracked members of execution squads, doctors who experimented on helpless prisoners, brutal camp guards. He also tracked the desk officers who kept the Nazi death machine running.

Wiesenthal's passion for justice brought many Nazis to account for their deeds. Perhaps just as important, his work kept the memory of the Holocaust alive. It reminded good people that they should not allow any group to be killed or persecuted. It put war criminals on notice that justice could catch up with them at any time. "I see what I'm doing as a warning to the murderers of tomorrow," Wiesenthal told a journalist. "A warning to them that they will never rest in peace."[3]

Chapter

1 Ordinary Dreams

Simon Wiesenthal was born shortly before midnight on December 31, 1908, in the town of Buczacz, which was then part of Austria. His grandparents believed that the first Jewish child of a new year would be especially blessed. To please them, Simon's parents delayed reporting the birth until January 1. Officially, the son of Asher and Rosa Wiesenthal was the first baby of 1909.

A BOY OF BUCZACZ

Young Simon came into a world that was overwhelmingly Jewish. Of the nine thousand inhabitants in Buczacz, six thousand were Jews.[4] In many other towns of the province called Galicia, Jews lived as a despised minority. In Buczacz, as Simon often said, "a Jew could hold his head up high."

The Wiesenthals were traditional Jews, steeped in the lore of their religious and cultural traditions. They spoke Yiddish (the language of Eastern European Jews), observed Jewish customs, accepted Jewish values. Simon was never self-conscious about being Jewish. He accepted it the way he accepted his gender and his parentage. It was a fact of life that defined

him and his place in the world. That grounding in Jewish identity would serve him well in the years to come.

Simon and his younger brother Hillel enjoyed being typical Jewish boys in a typical Jewish home. They looked forward to holidays, especially the eight-day Passover celebration, which began with a seder. At this traditional meal, Jews use song and story to retell the ancient tale of Moses' leading the Jews out of slavery in Egypt. Simon's favorite part of the seder was watching for the prophet Elijah.

Elijah, it was said, never tasted death. He was taken alive into heaven to watch over the Jewish people. Often he walked among them in disguise, helping a needy person here, performing a quiet miracle there. Jewish families honored Elijah by setting out a goblet of wine for him. Legend had it that the prophet visited every home to take a sip of wine from his special cup.

Toward the end of the seder, the family would sing the plaintive *"Eliyahu ha-navi"* ("Elijah the Prophet") and open the front door for the prophet to enter. He never came, at least as far as Simon could see. The cup remained untouched.

Simon's grandmother insisted that Elijah did come. He came and he drank. The

An engraving of the ascent of Elijah.

Simon's grandmother often took him to visit one of these rabbis. On one such visit, Simon noticed a sad-faced man who never moved. He just sat there, staring out an attic window. Simon's grandmother told him the story.

This was "the silent one,"[6] the man who did not speak. Once, during an argument with his wife, the man had exclaimed, "[I] Wish you burnt." That very night, the house caught on fire and the woman burned to death. Though the husband had nothing to do with the fire, he was overcome by guilt. He asked a miracle rabbi what he should do to atone for his words.

The verdict might seem harsh by modern standards. The rabbi told the man that he should not speak again for the rest of his life. He should live in silence, praying endlessly for forgiveness. A friend of Simon's wrote: "This mystical concept of justice has remained with Wiesenthal to this day. [Wiesenthal believes] . . . that in each life there is a balance between crime and punishment. . . . Guilt cannot be forgiven but only paid for by expiation [atonement; making amends]."[7]

cup only appeared to be full because "He doesn't drink more than a tear."[5]

LEARNING ABOUT JUSTICE

The stories and legends of Jewish culture were very real to Simon's grandmother. Like many Jews of that time and place, she had connections to the Hasidim, the Jewish mystics who sought to know God through prayer and meditation. They believed that their rabbis (teachers) were sages (wise men) and wonder-workers.

ANOTHER WORLD

When Simon was seven, his life in Buczacz came to a sudden end. Austria was at war, fighting on the side of Germany in the bloody conflict that came to be known as World War I (June 1914–November 1918). Simon's father joined the Austrian army. On October 14, 1915, he was killed fighting on the Russian front.

The armies of the czar, the Russian emperor, crossed into Galicia and closed on Buczacz. Rosa Wiesenthal was frightened. She knew that anti-Semitic Russians sometimes slaughtered Jews in organized massacres called pogroms. She packed up her two children and her aging parents and fled to Vienna.

The family found an apartment in the Jewish quarter. It was a run-down neighborhood of dingy streets and shabby tenement buildings. The Jews who lived there were poor. To seven-year-old Simon, who had known only the measured rhythms of life in the shtetl, or small Jewish town, Vienna was a vast mystery.

He soon learned to like it. Never had he seen so many different kinds of people. In Buczacz, Simon had known only Jews who kept to the old ways. In Vienna, he went to school with Gentiles, played with them, and learned not to be afraid of their differences. He also met secular, or nonreligious, Jews who lived comfortably in the Gentile world.

After two years in bustling Vienna, Rosa Wiesenthal decided it would be safe to return home. The war was nearly over and the Russians had been forced out of Galicia. Rosa took Simon with her back to Buczacz. The rest of the family, including Simon's grandmother, who

THE RIGHTEOUS AMONG US

The tzaddik, *or righteous man, was an important figure in Simon Wiesenthal's childhood world. In "The Righteous Among Us," which appeared in the English-language Israeli newspaper,* The Jerusalem Post, *in September 1996, author Sue Fishkoff discusses this enduring figure of Jewish lore.*

"The *tzaddik* takes various forms, from the saintly Torah [biblical] scholar, to the wonder-working holy man, to the simple yet pious doer of good deeds venerated in the world of the shtetl.

Throughout Jewish history, the tzaddik has been accorded the kind of respect other cultures reserved for kings and warriors. Piety, kindness, humility and faith in God's goodness are the traditional hallmarks of the tzaddik. Whether learned or simple, miracle worker or dispenser of homespun advice, the tzaddik represents the path of righteousness. . . . Above all, the tzaddik is someone who inspires by personal example. . . . Tzaddikim have many virtues, notably piety, kindness, humility and unswerving faith in God's goodness. But the Jewish understanding of righteousness demands that one does good in order to be good."

THE PROPHET ELIJAH HEALS THE SICK

The lore of Eastern European Jews includes many tales of Elijah the prophet. In the popular imagination, he was a wonder-worker, moving through the Jewish world in disguise. As this story, taken from Joachim Neugroschel's The Shtetl *shows, one never knew where Elijah might turn up.*

"In a village, there lived a family: a father, a mother, and a son. The father was a poor tailor, he earned little and they lived poorly. The son helped a bit, and the mother did housework. One day, she fell ill and she lay in bed for a long time. There was no doctor. Once, in the middle of the day, an old man walked in and he asked them:
'Who is sick here? I will cure him.'
The father answered: 'I have nothing to pay you with.'
The old man answered: 'I will wait for the money.'
The father said: 'I don't have a penny to my name.'
The old man gave them a medicine and promptly vanished. The woman recovered. At night, when their son went to bed, he found a sack of gold. From then on, they lived in wealth. They realized that the old man was the prophet Elijah."

had been widowed in the spring of 1917, stayed in Vienna. Simon was miserable. He no longer felt at home in Buczacz. He missed his grandmother, his school friends, the life he had left behind in the city. To make things worse, his mother was working night and day to reestablish her husband's sugar wholesaling business. Rosa had to contact suppliers and former customers, learning the business as she went along. She had no time to listen to the troubles of a bored and lonely nine-year-old boy.

Because Simon was so unhappy, his mother sent him back to his grandmother in Vienna. When Rosa finished getting the business on its feet, she brought the whole family home to Buczacz. Simon's life in Vienna had

become a thing of the past. He had no choice but to get used to Buczacz all over again.

HARD TIMES IN BUCZACZ

Very briefly, life appeared to settle into the old pattern. But in November 1917, Russian revolutionaries overthrew the czar and established a communist government. The next year, Austria was defeated in World War I and lost Galicia. The province then became a battleground between Russia and Poland.

It was a time of uncertainty and fear among the Jews of Buczacz: "We would get up [in the morning] without knowing which regime was in power,"[8] Simon Wiesenthal told one of his biographers.

He did not mean that literally, of course. Wiesenthal has a storyteller's flair for the dramatic. He often uses hyperbole—exaggerations not meant to be taken literally—to dramatize an incident or drive home a point.

At the age of twelve, Simon was attacked by a drunken cossack, a Russian peasant soldier. He was crossing the street in front of his house when the mounted soldier came thundering down on him. As the cossack passed the terrified boy, he lashed out with his sword. Simon fell, screaming, his thigh cut through to the bone.

The injury left a permanent scar. In later life, Simon Wiesenthal would say that the scar served as a reminder: Nazis were not the only brutal anti-Semites in the world. Hatred wore many faces. Any justice worthy of the name could neither condemn nor excuse an entire group. Real justice must hold individuals responsible for their personal actions.

THE LEARNING YEARS

In 1923, fifteen-year-old Simon entered high school. Though he was bright and gifted with a nearly photographic memory, he was not a particularly good student. He paid more attention to a pretty blonde classmate named Cyla Müller than he did to his teachers.

He also liked to draw. He enjoyed it so much that he would sometimes skip classes to stay home and work in his sketchbook. Though his sketches showed a definite talent, the family probably did not encourage Simon's artistic interests. Young people who did not come from

Simon (center) and a group of Boy Scouts, of which he was the leader and only camp survivor.

wealthy homes were expected to train for a practical occupation—and that did not include art.

While Simon was struggling with adolescence, tragedy struck the family. His thirteen-year-old brother, Hillel, broke his back in a freak accident. Rosa Wiesenthal took her youngest son to a specialist in Vienna, but there was nothing to be done. The boy was completely paralyzed. He died a few months later. The family was still struggling with that grief when Simon's beloved grandmother also died. Suddenly, Simon and his mother found themselves alone in the world.

They tried to help one another, but they were not particularly close. As a widow, Rosa had been so busy trying to make a living that she left Simon to his own devices. In 1926, she remarried and moved away from Buczacz to be with her new husband. Simon wanted to stay and finish high school, so his mother arranged for him to board with Cyla Müller's parents.

Simon and Cyla were high school sweethearts. Nearly everybody in Buczacz assumed they would get married; they were obviously very much in love. There was only one obstacle to a wedding. By the standards of the time, Simon had to demonstrate his ability to support a wife before he could propose to Cyla.

For her sake he cast aside his youthful dream of becoming an artist and decided to study architecture. Finding a school that would accept him proved to be a problem. The university in the nearby city of Lvov (also known as Lwów and Lembeck) would not accept Jews into the architectural program.

Simon had to go to Prague, Czechoslovakia, to find a school that would take him. That proved to be a blessing in disguise. Prague stretched Simon's horizons. Living in that thousand-year-old city was much like living in Vienna. Now that he was an adult, Simon could truly appreciate the rich cultural diversity. In Prague, he saw beyond the narrow world of the shtetl to a way of life where opportunities abounded. He liked what he saw.

BUILDING A LIFE

In 1932, Simon left Prague with his degree in architecture. Though this was a major achievement, he was only halfway to his goal. Before he could be certified in Poland, he needed a Polish diploma. To get it, he applied to the Technical University in Lvov. This time, the university allowed him to enroll as a part-time student despite its policies against Jews.

The postgraduate stay in Lvov was not a happy time. In 1932, Adolf Hitler and his Nazis were on the verge of taking over the government of Germany and anti-Semitism was on the rise in much of Eastern Europe. In Lvov, Jewish university students were harassed and sometimes attacked.

Just walking to the campus could be dangerous. Often Jewish students had to run a gauntlet between two lines of people who struck at them with various sorts of weapons, clubs, and whips. Some used sticks tipped with razor blades.

In addition to this unofficial harassment, the university had "Jew-free days." On these days, Jewish students were forbidden to enter the campus. Often, "Jew-free days" were declared during examination periods, and thus prevented Jewish students from qualifying for their degrees.

Even without his certification, Wiesenthal began receiving architectural commissions from well-to-do members of Lvov's Jewish community. In September 1936, he decided he was well enough established in his chosen profession to ask for Cyla's hand in marriage.

Simon Wiesenthal and Cyla Müller took their vows in a proper Jewish wedding on September 9, 1936. The newlyweds settled in Lvov, where Simon continued his work and his studies. Those early days of marriage were a strange time for the young couple. On the one hand, they were happy to be together and to have all of life ahead of them. They dreamed the usual dreams of young married people. They wanted a home, a family, a happy and prosperous future. On the other hand, they could not ignore what was happening in Germany and all around them.

Wiesenthal and his wife, Cyla, shortly before the outbreak of World War II.

THE NIGHTMARE BEGINS

Adolf Hitler was by this time both president and chancellor (secretary of state) of Germany. His National Socialist, or Nazi, Party controlled Germany's government, its economy, and its social institutions. Already there were rumors of war. Germany needed *lebensraum* (living space), Hitler had said. The logical place for expansion lay in the neighboring countries of Eastern Europe.

Germany had already annexed Austria and occupied the Rhineland, the province west of the Rhine River. The whole world was waiting to see what would happen next.

On March 15, 1939, Germany invaded Czechoslovakia. They took over the country by browbeating and blackmailing its leaders. The German army didn't have to fight a single battle. Journalist William Shirer called the taking of Czechoslovakia "one of the most brazen [bold, shameless] acts of [Hitler's] entire career."[9]

Six months later, on August 23, 1939, Hitler signed a nonaggression pact with Soviet dictator Josef Stalin. The two leaders

WHAT IS ANTI-SEMITISM?

Although the term "anti-Semitism" did not exist until 1879, the hatred of Jews it describes is much older. In Facing History and Ourselves, *Strom and Parsons quote Yehuda Bauer on the reasons for anti-Semitism.*

"One reason [for this hatred] was the mounting religious fanaticism and superstition of Christians; another was that Jews were in effect forced by Christians into the unpopular but necessary money-lending business, because the Church in those days forbade Christians to charge interest.

From the time of the Crusades, Jews were forced to live separately in ghettos. Popular hostility often erupted into violence. Forced conversion, pillage, expulsion and even massacre became common, sometimes inspired as much by a desire to get rid of inconvenient creditors [persons to whom money is owed] as by religious zealotry. Persecution grew still worse with the Black Death, a vast plague epidemic in 1348–51, which popular superstition blamed on the Jews."

In his magazine article "The Face of Modern Anti-Semitism," *author Richard Hecht discusses historian Leon Poliakov's ideas about the three main expressions of anti-Semitism:*

"[It] appears in the context of social and political distinctions; it has [religious] characteristics; and it necessitates some racial distinction. In various historical periods one of these expressions becomes dominant. So, Poliakov characterizes the anti-Semitism of late antiquity [late Roman Empire] as social or political; the anti-Semitism of the Middle Ages as [religious]; and the anti-Semitism of the modern world as racial. The dominance of one form does not mean that the others are not present, but only that they [are of lesser importance than] the dominant expression."

An anti-Semitic poster urging Germans not to buy from Jewish vendors.

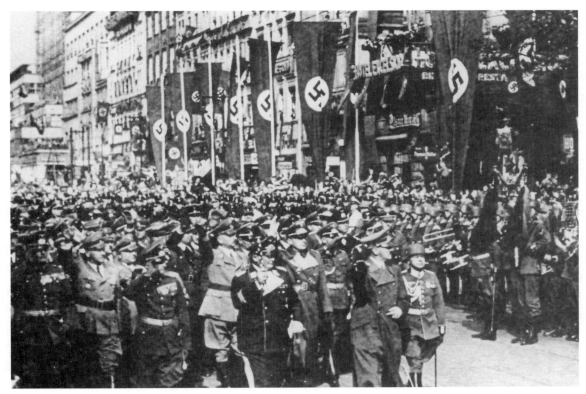

Adolf Hitler's German army occupies the Czech Sudetenland in 1938.

agreed to split Poland between them. This left Germany free to attack without fear of Russian reprisals. On September 1, 1939, Hitler's troops did just that, and World War II began.

In that same year, Simon Wiesenthal finally completed his Polish diploma. He had achieved a longstanding goal only to find that it no longer mattered. Germany controlled western Poland. The Soviet Union controlled the east, including Galicia.

When the Communists took Galicia, they arrested Jewish merchants, doctors, lawyers, and teachers for the "crime" of being members of the propertied middle class. Wiesenthal's stepfather, who owned a brick factory, was one of the first to be arrested. After the NKVD (Soviet Security Police) took him into custody, the family never saw him again. He died in a Soviet prison. Wiesenthal's mother, widowed for a second time, moved in with her son and daughter-in-law.

Once more, the family faced hard times. The Soviet authorities issued special identity cards to Jews and would not allow them to live in the larger cities. By bribing an NKVD official, Wiesenthal was able to get regular papers for himself, Cyla, and his mother. This allowed them to remain in Lvov.

At the time, Simon simply wanted to stay where he could find some job. Only later did he realize the true importance of those unrestricted papers. Jews without them were rounded up and exiled to Siberia. Hundreds died in this harsh environment—of cold and exposure, of starvation, of disease. That bribe to the NKVD may well have saved the Wiesenthal family's lives.

Despite his Polish diploma, the Soviets would not allow Wiesenthal to work as an architect. After all his years of schooling, he ended up making down bedcovers in a small factory. The family squeaked by, living from hand to mouth and day to day. Bad as this was, the worst was yet to come.

On June 22, 1941, Hitler cast aside the pact he had made with Stalin. German troops invaded Soviet-occupied Poland. On June 28, they marched into Lvov. The Jews of Lvov had fallen into the hands of a government that meant to exterminate them.

Chapter

2 Unthinkable Things

The Nazis secured Lvov with the help of Ukrainian collaborators whose hatred of Jews very nearly matched their own. The Ukrainians launched a pogrom that lasted three days and left six thousand Jews dead.

A Close Call

This slaughter was followed by mass arrests of Jewish intellectuals and business-people. The Nazis used the telephone directory and other sources to identify educated, middle-class Jews who might stir up trouble in the community. Dozens were grabbed off the streets or pulled from their homes. Ukrainian collaborators found Simon Wiesenthal hiding in a basement and hauled him off to Brigidki prison.

They did not even bother to put him in a cell. Wiesenthal found himself in a courtyard with a group of about forty Jews. The police lined them up against a wall, and placed a wooden crate next to each person. Then they started down the line, shooting each victim in the neck and dumping his body into the crate. They were almost to Wiesenthal when the church bells rang, calling the faithful to vespers (an evening church service).

The Ukrainians agreed to postpone the rest of the executions until morning. They put the surviving victims into prison cells and went off to say their evening prayers.

Wiesenthal went to sleep expecting to die come sunrise. Instead, he was awakened in the middle of the night by a friendly voice. It was a Pole named Bodnar; Wiesenthal had once done him a favor. Though Bodnar wore the armband of the Ukrainian auxiliary, Wiesenthal described him as a "decent, honest man."[10]

He was also a clever one. He got Wiesenthal out of the prison by denouncing him as a Soviet spy. Bodnar claimed he had orders to take Wiesenthal to the commissar's office for questioning. Fortunately, nobody checked these orders. Bodnar left with his "prisoner" in tow. Before dawn, Wiesenthal was back in his own home. Thanks to Bodnar, he had slipped through the cracks of the system. For the moment, he was safe. It was the first of a "succession of miracles"[11] that enabled him to survive the war.

Life in the Ghetto

The Nazis forced the Jews of Lvov to leave their homes and move into a ghetto,

A homeless family huddles on a street in the Warsaw ghetto.

a run-down neighborhood in which they would be isolated from the rest of the town. The Jews themselves had to build the fence. They also had to pull up the cobblestones, turning the streets "into a quagmire. . . . On rainy days you couldn't cross the street without wading in mud up to your ankles," Wiesenthal said. "It was impossible to clean oneself. We must have looked like animals, or phantoms."[12] It was all part of the Nazi plan to make the ghetto as unlivable as possible.

People were packed into tiny apartments, sometimes as many as seven to a room. Most of them were slowly starving to death. The daily food allotment generally amounted to two or three slices of bread and a bowl of watery soup per person. Jews were forced to exist on as little as six hundred calories a day.

LIFE IN A LABOR CAMP

On October 21, 1941, the SS (*Schutzstaffel*; a secret police unit) selected people from the ghetto for slave labor. Simon and Cyla were assigned to the Janowskà labor camp. Before they left, Simon gave his mother a gold watch. He told her to use it as a bribe if anyone came to take her away.

In the camp, the prisoners quarried stone and did other heavy work. At the end of each day, anyone who looked sick was not allowed to return to the barracks. He or she had to sleep outside on the frozen ground. In subzero temperatures, this was a death sentence. The Germans called it a "fresh-air cure."[13]

No one lasted in the Janowskà camp for long. Every morning, the living dug burial pits for the dead. Sooner or later, the Wiesenthals would have been among the dead except for what biographer Hella Pick called "a mini-miracle."[14] Both Cyla and Simon were transferred to the railway repair works.

THE GOOD NAZIS

Heinrich Günthert and his assistant Adolf Kohlrautz were the most unusual Nazis Wiesenthal had ever met. They did not mistreat their Jewish prisoners. Every worker got decent food and decent treatment. Günthert had already been in trouble with his superiors for "coddling" Jews. Even that did not change his attitude.

Günthert put Simon to work painting German eagles and Nazi swastikas on captured locomotives. Cyla polished brass fittings in a railway engine plant.

Wiesenthal never told the Germans that he was an architect. He claimed he was simply a man with a knack for drawing. When Günthert discovered his swastika-painter's secret, he demanded to know why Wiesenthal had not told him the truth. A Jew caught lying to a German official could be shot where he stood. Wiesenthal did not know what to do. Günthert stood staring at him, waiting for an answer.

Nazi or not, Günthert seemed to be a decent man. Wiesenthal decided to give him an honest answer—that he figured he would stay alive longer by hiding his profession. Simon's explanation had the ring of truth, and Günthert knew it. He "walked up and down," for a while, Wiesenthal remembered. "Then he called Adolf Kohlrautz, his deputy. They decided to give me work as a [draftsman]."[15]

The new job brought even more privileges. Kohlrautz gave Wiesenthal a private hut for his work. Soon he lived there

A mass of Jewish bodies lie frozen on the ground.

Hitler's Followers: What They Said About the Führer

In his book Hitler Warned Us, *author John Laffin quotes important Nazis showing their reverence for Adolf Hitler:*

"There are two types of speaker. One just speaks, the other speaks from the heart. This is Adolf Hitler. He speaks spontaneously and therefore people understand and trust him. Men think it is magic when Hitler speaks. I heard somebody say, 'Hitler is Columbus! A great discoverer with much knowledge.' He is the first to speak to the German people about unemployment and jobs and he reached the soul of the German people with that speech."

— Joseph Goebbels,
Minister of Propaganda

"It is with pride that we see that one man is kept above all criticism—the Führer. The reason is that everybody feels and knows he was right and will always be right. The National Socialism of us all is anchored in . . . uncritical loyalty [and] devotion to the Führer."

— Rudolf Hess,
Head of the Chancellery

"How shall I give expression, O my Führer, to what is in our hearts? How shall I find words to express your deeds? Has there ever been a mortal as beloved as you, my Führer? Was there ever belief as strong as the belief in your mission? You were sent up by God for Germany!"

— Hermann Göring,
Supreme Commander of the Luftwaffe

as well, and did not have to go back to the barracks at Janowskà. Kohlrautz even arranged for Cyla to join her husband. For a time, the young couple lived almost normally.

Wiesenthal did not for a moment forget his situation. He still expected to be pulled back to Janowskà, or deported to someplace even worse. He had heard of camps where people were gassed by the hundreds, even the thousands. Many Jews did not want to believe that such places existed. It was a rumor, they claimed, nothing more.

In the summer of 1942, that "rumor" came to terrible life. The SS swept through the ghetto, rounding up people who were too old or sick to work. Rosa Wiesenthal was one of those people.

Decades later, Wiesenthal still got a catch in his voice when he talked about his mother's fate: "A neighbor told us that a Ukrainian policeman had come, and that my mother had tried to buy her life with the gold watch. But half an hour later, another policeman came. And she had nothing left with which to buy her freedom."[16]

The SS sent Rosa Wiesenthal to the Belzec extermination camp. Simon and Cyla never saw her again.

STRANGE DESTINIES

Wiesenthal could not save his mother from the Nazi death machine. But early in 1943, he managed to get his wife out of

Hundreds of corpses of death camp inmates fill the streets.

HITLER'S ORDERS FOR THE INVASION OF POLAND

In this statement to his officers, quoted by Strom and Parsons in Facing History and Ourselves, *Hitler reveals the evil intent and distorted vision for which he became infamous.*

"Our strength is in our quickness and brutality. Ghengis Khan had millions of women and children killed by his own will and with a [happy] heart. History has seen only in him a great state builder. What weak Western European civilization thinks about me does not matter. . . . I have sent to the east only my 'Death Head units' with the order to kill without mercy all men, women and children of Polish race or language. Only in such a way will we win the vital [living] space we need."

German troops enter Poland in 1939.

harm's way. Cyla Wiesenthal did not look Jewish. With her blonde hair and gray-blue eyes, she could easily pass for a Pole. She spoke the language fluently and had been around enough Gentiles to know how to behave. All she needed was fake identification and someone to shelter her.

Because of his work at the railway yard, Wiesenthal met several members of the Polish underground. He made a deal with them; he would give them maps of key railway points if they would take his wife to safety. The Polish freedom-fighters agreed. They would smuggle Cyla out of camp and find her lodgings. The one thing they could not do was get Polish papers for her.

For that, Wiesenthal turned to his unlikely friend, Adolf Kohlrautz. Without mentioning the Polish freedom-fighters, he explained what he wanted to do. Kohlrautz scarcely blinked an eye. He handed over a blank identity form and told Wiesenthal to pick a suitable Polish name. Then he turned his back so Wiesenthal could forge the official signature, while Kohlrautz officially knew nothing about it.

As "Irena Kowalska," Cyla Wiesenthal went to the city of Lubin, where she lived with the family of a Polish architect. Later, she moved to Warsaw, where she found work in a radio factory and settled down to the life of a Polish woman in occupied Warsaw.

For some time, the Wiesenthals were able to keep in touch. Simon could telephone Cyla from his office in the railway works. They lost touch when the Gestapo, the dreaded SS security police, rounded up

Polish women to work in a machine gun factory. "Irena Kowalska" spent the last years of the war in a forced-labor barracks. Had the Nazis known she was Jewish, they would have sent her to a death camp.

While Cyla was trying to survive as a Pole, Simon faced dangers of his own. On April 20, 1943, the commandant of the Janowskà camp decided to celebrate Adolf Hitler's fifty-fourth birthday by killing fifty-four Jewish intellectuals. He had already killed so many educated Jews that he could not find enough suitable victims. He ordered a roundup of people working outside the camp. An SS man appeared at the railway works to take Wiesenthal and two others back to Janowskà.

At the camp, laughing guards made the prisoners strip naked and walk down "the pipe."[17] This was a narrow corridor of barbed wire fencing which led to a sandpit at the far end. As each prisoner reached the pit, an SS executioner fired one machine gun burst. The victim fell forward into the sand. In time, the bodies would sink out of sight.

Walking down the pipe, Wiesenthal knew he was going to die. He watched the first executions almost calmly. There was nothing else to do. Anyone who panicked or begged or tried to run only gave the guards an excuse for more brutality: "Each of us was alone with himself, with his thoughts," Wiesenthal told writer Alan Levy. "Each was his own island of solitude."[18]

As Wiesenthal continued down the pipe a sound pierced his silence. It was

The Order that Created the Ghettos

When the Nazis invaded Poland in 1939, one of their first priorities was to deal with the "Jewish question." The order creating ghettos to be administered by Jewish councils was issued by Reinhard Heydrich of the SS. This partial text of that order can be found on the Internet at: http://library.advanced. org/ 12307/index.html

"SECRET
   Berlin: September 21, 1939
   To: Chiefs of all Einsatzgruppen of the Security Police
   Subject: Jewish question in the occupied territory
   I refer to the conference held in Berlin today. . . . For the time being, the first step toward the final goal is the concentration of the Jews from the countryside into the larger cities. This is to be carried out with all speed. . . . In each Jewish community, a Council of Jewish Elders is to be set up. . . .The councils of Elders are to be informed of the dates and deadlines. . . .They are then to be made personally responsible for the departure of the Jews from the countryside. . . .For general reasons of security, the concentration of Jews in the cities will probably necessitate orders altogether barring Jews from certain sections of the cities, or, for example, forbidding them to leave the ghetto. . . .
   [Signed] Heydrich"

Abandoned Jewish children in the Warsaw ghetto.

A Jewish man is discovered hiding in the floorboards of an old house.

the sound of his name; someone shouting his name. An SS corporal had come to get him. He was needed at the railway works, the corporal said. He had important work to do.

Wiesenthal dressed quickly and followed the corporal. From the pipe, he heard the sound of machine gun bursts, interrupted by brief periods of silence. He knew that the Nazis had probably grabbed another Jew to take his place. His good fortune was somebody else's death warrant. He tried not to think about it.

At the railway yard, a grinning Kohlrautz welcomed Wiesenthal back to the world of the living. The "important work" that only he could do was to paint a gigantic poster for the führer's (Adolf Hitler's) birthday celebration.

In the Third Reich, no Jew was safe for long. By September, rumors flew around the railway yard. Jewish workers would no longer be allowed to live outside Janowskà. The commandant planned to bring them back to camp. Wiesenthal knew that would be a death sentence.

Kohlrautz knew it, too. On October 2, 1943, he arranged for Wiesenthal and another Jewish worker, Arthur Scheiman, to go into town for supplies. He gave them a pass and assigned a Ukrainian who did not know the area to go along as their guard.

Slipping away was easy. Wiesenthal and Scheiman went into a stationery store, supposedly to buy art supplies. The guard waited outside. The two prisoners slipped out the back door and got away on a streetcar. Once free, the two men went their separate ways, although they would meet again.

Wiesenthal never saw Adolf Kohlrautz again, however. In later years, he would use Kohlrautz as an object lesson: all people, even Nazis, must be judged individually. When he needed to underline that point, he told about Kohlrautz, the Nazi who saved his life.

Kohlrautz himself died in 1945, fighting for his country in the Battle of Berlin.

LIVING ON THE RUN

Just a few weeks after Wiesenthal and Scheiman made their escape, the Nazis shut down most of Janowskà and killed its inmates. Some people managed to escape. The Nazis sent Ukrainian auxiliary police into the countryside to find them.

Wiesenthal had been staying with Polish friends who hid him in an attic. The manhunt for Janowskà escapees put him in new danger. It also endangered his Polish hosts. They could be executed for harboring Jews. Wiesenthal slipped away from the house and made his way to a partisan camp in the forest.

As a Jew, he had to be careful. There were several groups of partisans; some were nearly as anti-Semitic as the Nazis they fought. Wiesenthal found a friendly group and stayed with them as long as possible. That turned out to be February, 1944, when Nazi troops and Ukrainian auxiliaries began hunting for the rebels.

Wiesenthal and some of the others managed to slip through the lines and make their way into town. They went to the home of an underground operative who was loyal to the Allies—British, American, and Russian troops fighting Nazi Germany. He was also anti-Semitic, though under the circumstances he would allow Wiesenthal to stay with his Gentile companions.

Rather than trust his fate to a known anti-Semite, Wiesenthal set off on his own. He linked up again with Arthur Scheiman, who was hiding with his Gentile wife. Mrs. Scheiman was Ukrainian by birth, a seamstress by trade. She hid the two men in the closet of her workroom. They huddled in a dark corner behind Mrs. Scheiman's garments. Customers came for their fittings without the slightest idea that two fugitives hid behind their new dresses.

After about eight days, everybody involved in this dangerous scheme had thought better of it. Wiesenthal took Scheiman with him back to the partisans. Once more setting aside his anti-Semitism, the host agreed to shelter the Jews. The partisans dug a "grave" under the floorboards. When soldiers came to search the apartment, Wiesenthal and Scheiman lay down in their hiding place. The others replaced the floorboards and set a large table over the grave.

Scheiman considered this arrangement even worse than his wife's closet. He decided to return home and take his chances. Wiesenthal stayed. The procedure worked well enough until a group of Poles beat and robbed a German railway inspector in a nearby apartment. The Gestapo ordered a house-to-house search for the assailants.

HITLER IN HIS OWN WORDS

In Mein Kampf, *Adolf Hitler describes the beginning of his anti-Semitism, which he traces to his first encounter with an ultra-Orthodox Eastern European Jew.*

Nazi Germany's führer, Adolf Hitler.

"Once, as I was strolling through the Inner City [of Vienna, Austria], I suddenly encountered an apparition in a black caftan and black hair locks. Is this a Jew? Was my first thought.

For, to be sure, they had not looked like that in Linz. I observed the man furtively and cautiously, but the longer I stared at this foreign face, scrutinizing feature for feature, the more my first question assumed a new form:

Is this a German?

As always in such cases, I now began to try to relieve my doubts by books. For a [small sum] I bought the first anti-Semitic pamphlets of my life. . . . I could no longer very well doubt that [the Jews] were not Germans of a special religion, but a people in themselves; for since I had begun to concern myself with this question . . . Vienna appeared to me in a different light than before. Wherever I went, I began to see Jews, and the more I saw, the more sharply they became distinguished in my eyes from the rest of humanity."

The Polish partisans escaped just ahead of the Gestapo, but they left Wiesenthal trapped in the "grave." On June 13, 1944, two Polish policemen took up the floorboards and discovered the fugitive. Wiesenthal had two guns and a diary with him. Fortunately, his captors turned in the diary and kept the guns for themselves. If they had turned in the guns, Wiesenthal would have been executed at once—the penalty for Jews caught with firearms.

The diary interested the Gestapo. It included maps and diagrams coded so only Wiesenthal could read them. With a draftsman's attention to detail, he had charted the locations of partisan groups. He had meant the maps to guide the Soviet Red Army to people who would help them liberate Poland. Instead, they had fallen into the hands of Nazis, who would stop at nothing to find out their meaning.

Wiesenthal fully expected to be tortured for the information. He knew the Gestapo methods all too well. If they tortured him, he would break. Nobody held out forever. Sooner or later, he would betray his comrades. He decided that the only honorable thing to do was kill himself before he could be questioned.

A TIME TO DIE

In a world of death and hatred, suicide should have been easy. It was not. The Nazis had a reason for keeping Wiesenthal alive. They were determined that he should not die until it suited their purposes.

Wiesenthal was among a truckload of prisoners taken to what was left of Janowskà. It was a convenient place for housing prisoners the SS did not want to keep in town. Wiesenthal had been in Janowskà for only two days when the Gestapo came to get him.

To his horror, Wiesenthal found himself in the clutches of Master Sergeant Oskar Waltke, the most feared Gestapo man in all Galicia. Waltke was not satisfied with simply killing his victims. He liked to torture them first, even when they had no important information.

He especially liked to make Jews with false papers admit that they were Jews. "He tortured his victims until they con-

fessed and then he sent them to be shot," Wiesenthal said. "He also tortured many Gentiles until they admitted to being Jews just to get it over with."[19]

Waltke smiled as he loaded Wiesenthal into the van, a smile that was truly terrible to see. Reacting quickly, Wiesenthal grabbed a razor blade he had hidden in his cuff and slit both wrists with swift, deep strokes. He slumped to the floor, unconscious.

He came to in a prison hospital, with his wrists neatly bandaged and a doctor standing at his side. Wiesenthal was stunned. Jews who got sick or injured were not taken to the doctor. The Nazis either shot them or left them to die on their own.

If Wiesenthal missed the significance of this treatment, Waltke soon appeared to remind him. As soon as he recovered, they would be having a long talk. Wiesenthal was in the hospital for five weeks. During that time, Waltke made regular visits. He never failed to mention the "long talk" that lay ahead.

Twice more, Wiesenthal tried to cheat Waltke of his prize. He took a massive overdose of what turned out to be sugar pills, and then tried to hang himself with his belt. When those efforts failed, he became fatalistic and accepted that events could not be avoided or changed. He would accept whatever came. He had no other choice.

THE SS ON THE RUN

As it happened, fate had some surprises in store. Wiesenthal recovered in spite of himself and Waltke gleefully set the date for the interrogation: July 18, 1944. On that very day, Soviet planes bombed the area, sending prisoners and SS men alike scurrying in all directions. As Soviet cannons and field guns bombarded Lvov, the SS loaded the Jewish prisoners onto trucks and took them back to Janowskà. There began one of the strangest episodes of Wiesenthal's life.

The SS men fled before the advancing Red Army. Instead of killing the thirty-four Jews who remained alive in Janowskà, they took them along. By claiming to be guarding the prisoners, they hoped to stay out of combat. Fully two hundred SS men guarded the thirty-four surviving Jews of Janowskà.

The journey began on a train. When the tracks ended, the SS commandeered thirty horse-drawn wagons from a group of German civilians who were also fleeing the Soviet advance. One or two Jews and half a dozen SS men rode in each wagon. This "cowardly caravan,"[20] as writer Alan Levy called it, made its way to a field near the Polish city of Grybow. There they made camp. The SS had Wiesenthal paint a sign: "SS Construction Staff Venus." The idea was to look like an official military installation.

The ruse worked until Soviet troops closed on Grybow. Then the SS pulled up stakes and moved still farther to the west. The odyssey of Construction Staff Venus ended at the Plaszow concentration camp near the city of Cracow. There, a general unmasked the Venus project for what it was: a hoax designed to keep the SS men away from the Russian front. He

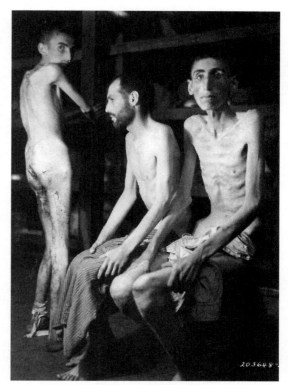

Emaciated survivors of the Buchenwald death camp at its liberation.

promptly dissolved the unit and sent the SS men into combat.

THE DYING REICH

After the SS left, the Jews of Construction Staff Venus were sent to work in the Gross Rosen rock quarry. It was there Wiesenthal heard that his wife was dead. In August 1944, the SS brought a group of new prisoners to the quarry. They were not Jews, but Poles from Warsaw who had dared to fight the German troops occupying their city. Wiesenthal found a man who had lived two doors down from Cyla's last known address. He asked the new arrival if he knew a woman named Irena Kowalska.

Yes, said the Pole, he knew Irena. She died in a German attack. "My friend, *no one in Topiel Street survived.* The Germans surrounded one house after another with flame-throwers and afterwards blew up what was left of the houses."[21]

In his writings and public statements, Wiesenthal has said little about his feelings at that moment. Many Holocaust survivors have spoken of being emotionally blunted during their ordeal. Normal grief sometimes got buried beneath ongoing despair. Wiesenthal believed what his informant told him, that there was no hope for "Irena Kowalska."

WAITING FOR THE END

At the beginning of 1945, the Red Army neared Gross Rosen. Once more, the SS fled with their prisoners, this time to the Buchenwald concentration camp. Wiesenthal was not there for long. The Germans were truly on the run by this time. Everywhere, Allied troops pressed toward the heart of the Third Reich.

In February, three thousand prisoners were taken out of Buchenwald. For six days, they traveled in a convoy of open trucks, without food or water. Eighteen hundred people died by the time the convoy reached the concentration camp Mauthausen.

Simon Wiesenthal was one of the survivors—but just barely. His six-foot, 180-pound frame had been reduced to a skeletal 90 pounds. He had a badly infected wound on one foot. The camp personnel put him into a barracks and left him to die.

Once more, Wiesenthal's drawing ability saved his life. A man named Eduard Staniszewski came to the barracks looking for someone to draw a birthday greeting for a coworker.

Wiesenthal did the drawing and received a piece of bread and a small sausage for his work. Other projects followed; each brought by Staniszewski, each accompanied by a reward of food. The extra food literally saved Wiesenthal's life. Without it, he would have starved before American troops liberated the camp.

During those last days, Wiesenthal spent much of his time drawing. He drew cartoon-style illustrations that captured the raw horror of the camp. Some of these were later collected into a book, *KZ Mauthausen; KZ* are the German initials for "concentration camp."

He also did a lot of thinking, sorting through memories that jumbled together in his mind. He knew liberation was close at hand, but he also knew he might not live long enough to see it. Either way, he needed to make some kind of sense out of all that had happened to him.

JUSTICE AND FORGIVENESS

One incident stood out in Wiesenthal's mind and even haunted his dreams. It had happened at the Lvov Technical University, where he had worked so hard for his Polish diploma. The campus had been converted into a Red Cross hospital.

Prisoners of the Mauthausen death camp cheer for their Allied liberators.

Wiesenthal was part of a prisoner detail assigned to work on the grounds. He was sneaking a moment's rest when a nurse hurried up to him. "Are you a Jew?" she asked.

Wiesenthal nodded.

"Come with me," she said. The nurse led Wiesenthal into the room that had once been the dean's office. It was a hospital room now. In the dim light, Wiesenthal could just make out the form of a patient lying in a white bed. The nurse murmured something to the man, then left the room. Wiesenthal stood there, not knowing what to do.

"Please come nearer, I can't speak loudly," the patient said.

Wiesenthal moved closer:

> Now I could see the figure in the bed far more clearly. White, bloodless hands on the [coverlet], head completely bandaged with openings only for mouth, nose, and ears. . . . It was an uncanny situation: those corpse-like hands, the bandages, and the place in which this strange encounter was taking place.[22]

The patient was a twenty-one-year-old SS soldier whom Wiesenthal identified only as "Karl." He was dying and he knew it. He wanted to clear his conscience before the end, he said. To do that, he needed to talk with a Jew.

While Wiesenthal perched uncomfortably on the edge of the bed, Karl told his story. He was part of an SS unit assigned to round up Jews in the Ukrainian city of Dnyepropetrovsk. They did their job with brutal efficiency. They gathered the city's four hundred Jews into a wooden house, then set the building on fire.

In all that horror, one image burned itself into the young soldier's mind. In an upstairs window, he saw a father with his clothes on fire, holding a child in his arms. The mother stood behind them. In an instant that seemed to last forever, the man shielded his son's eyes, then leaped from the window with the child held tightly in his arms. The mother followed: "I don't know how many tried to jump out of the windows but that one family I shall never forget—least of all the child. It had black hair and dark eyes."[23] The dying soldier fell silent, lost perhaps in his own fevered memories.

Wiesenthal was also captured by a memory, a memory of sunflowers in a German military cemetery. Each grave had one of the tall, colorful blossoms that always turn their faces to the sun. They symbolized honor and connected the dead to the life they had left behind. Jews did not have sunflowers on their graves. They lay in anonymous pits or heaps of ashes, unhonored, unremembered, unmourned.

After Karl had told his story, he begged for a word of forgiveness. "I know what I am asking is almost too much for you, but without your answer I cannot die in peace."[24]

Wiesenthal could not bring himself to speak. In the Jewish tradition, forgiveness must come from the victim. No one else has the right to offer it. Wiesenthal sat for a time in silence, then walked out of the room without saying a word.

Had he done the right thing? That was the question he asked his friends at Janowskà, and asked himself at Mauthausen as he lay waiting for death or liberation. It was still tugging at his mind on May 5, 1945, when American tanks rolled into Mauthausen and the long nightmare came to an end.

Chapter

3 A World We Never Made

Liberation brought its own uncertainties. The world Simon Wiesenthal had known lay in ashes. His family was dead. Half-starved and numb with grief, he could not bring himself to rejoice over being alive.

People he did not know tried to cheer him. The horror was over, they said. He could soon go back to his life. Go back? Impossible. Architecture no longer had any meaning for him. Somehow Wiesenthal knew even then that his experiences in the Holocaust would shape the rest of his days.

RETURN TO THE WORLD OF THE LIVING

Wiesenthal has never forgotten how he looked when the Americans came to Mauthausen: "[M]y face was no more than a bony triangle around [my eyes], with skin stretched tight and a mouth that was an open wound."[25]

He had been living on a starvation diet for so long that a bowl of hearty soup made him sick to his stomach. Some survivors actually died because they ate more than their digestive systems could handle. The Americans began feeding them more carefully. They started each person out with thin soup and bread and slowly worked up to more solid foods.

The Americans cleaned and disinfected the barracks. They buried the dead and cared for the living. Wiesenthal was just getting used to decent treatment when a fellow survivor beat him senseless. His attacker was Kazimierz Rusinek, a Polish barracks clerk. Rusinek was working for the Americans. He was supposed to be keeping things in order and helping fellow survivors adjust to freedom.

Part of his job was giving passes for people to leave camp. When Wiesenthal asked for one, Rusinek flew into a rage: "He retorted that I would have been dead if the Nazis had still been there. Then he beat me up and threw me out into the courtyard."[26]

Wiesenthal could not tolerate being beaten by somebody who was supposed to help him. Though he could barely walk, he got two other prisoners to help him to the American commander's office. While Wiesenthal waited to make his report, he saw American soldiers bringing SS men in for questioning.

Slowly he realized what was happening; the Americans were establishing a war crimes office. They planned to investigate what the Nazis had done and hold individuals accountable for any crimes they had committed. There would be trials, testimonies, punishments. The world would learn what had happened in the ghettos and death camps of Nazi Germany. Wiesenthal watched and listened, hanging onto every word.

THE CALLING

The incident with Rusinek paled next to this. The next morning, Wiesenthal went back to the American commander's office. He no longer cared about bringing charges against Rusinek, he said. He wanted to help investigate Nazi war crimes.

> [Y]ou liberated, me, you saved my life. But I don't know what to do with my life. I have no one for whom or with whom I want to live. Now that I've seen what you're doing here in this office, I'd like to participate. That could be a task which would lend some meaning to my life. I spent four years in various concentration camps, in ghettos, and in Gestapo prisons. I've seen a lot and I have a good memory. I can help you find the criminals, put the right questions to them, [question] them. I don't expect any pay—I want to do it to justify my own survival.[27]

After this impassioned statement, Lieutenant Abby Mann asked a single question: "How much do you weigh?"

"A hundred and thirty pounds,"[28] Wiesenthal replied.

He did not weigh anywhere near 130, and Lieutenant Mann knew it. He told Wiesenthal that he was in no shape for such work. First, he had to get healthy. In the meantime, he could write a letter, explaining the facts as he remembered them.

Wiesenthal set about the task with a vengeance. Calling upon his memory skills, he began making lists. By the time he finished, he had ninety-one names, along with dates, places, and a description of their crimes. He had the exact address of the railway agent who shot an elderly woman "before my eyes."[29] He had Frederich Warzog, the Janowskà commander who used Jews as a human shield in the retreat from the Allies. He had Leo John of Plasgow, who specialized in killing women and children. He also had Amon Göth, the Plasgow commandant whose crimes would be detailed in the movie *Schindler's List*.

When Wiesenthal was finished he returned to Lieutenant Mann. Again, he asked if he could join the War Crimes unit. "'Of course,' [Mann] said. 'You've been with us for a long time already.'"[30]

WIESENTHAL ON PATROL

Though still weak and underweight, Wiesenthal threw himself into his new role as Nazi hunter. He was assigned to an American captain. Together, the two men searched the countryside around Mauthausen, looking for former camp guards in hiding. They found plenty.

LIBERATING THE CAMPS

When Allied troops liberated the Nazi concentration camps, nothing had prepared them for the horror they saw. General Dwight D. Eisenhower sent for American newspaper editors to document the atrocities. Joseph Pulitzer II of the St. Louis Post-Dispatch *filed the following report on April 29, 1945.*

"As one of a group of newspaper and magazine editors, I was invited by Gen. Eisenhower to . . . inspect the concentration camp at Buchenwald, near Weimar. We were flown there on April 25, the day after our arrival in Paris, and made a complete inspection of the camp. . . . I came here in a suspicious frame of mind, feeling that I would find that many of the terrible reports that have been printed in the United States before I left were exaggerations, and largely propaganda. . . .

It is my grim duty to report that the descriptions of the horrors of this camp, one of many which have been and which will be uncovered by the Allied armies have given less than the whole truth. They have been understatements. The brutal fiendishness of these operations defies description.

Photographs I have seen helped to tell the true story. . . . They are terrible to look at, and many readers will be shocked by them, but they are the true evidence of what went on. There can be no doubt but the black hole of Calcutta fades into insignificance when compared with the . . . murder factory of Buchenwald."

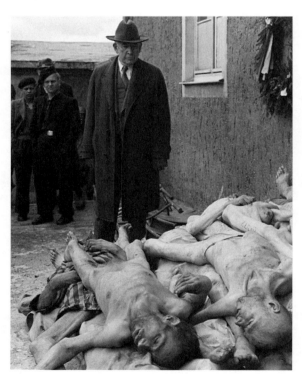

Bodies of Buchenwald victims lie unburied after the camp's liberation in 1945.

"You didn't have to go far," Wiesenthal remembers. "You almost stumbled over them." Wiesenthal was a relentless hunter. He identified the men for the Americans, and sometimes helped the captain make actual arrests. Finally, he made an arrest on his own; a former guard identified only as "Schmidt."

While the captain waited in the jeep, Wiesenthal climbed two flights of stairs to Schmidt's apartment. He was out of breath by the time he confronted one of his former tormentors. History does not record Schmidt's reaction when he found

Nazi officer Adolf Eichmann, the man who orchestrated the infamous "Final Solution."

himself face-to-face with the skeletal figure of Simon Wiesenthal.

He must have realized that his past had caught up with him. He did not try to escape. In fact, Weisenthal remembers that Schmidt actually helped him down the stairs and into the waiting jeep. On the way to American headquarters, the former SS guard broke into tears.

He was "only a little person," he said. He just obeyed orders. "I swear to you: I risked my own neck . . . to help prisoners."

Wiesenthal would hear that particular excuse many times. It never moved him: "Yes, you helped prisoners. I saw you often. You helped them on the way to the crematorium."[31]

The patrols around Mauthausen came to an abrupt end just three weeks after they started. The Americans, British, French, and Russians agreed to partition Austria into four military zones. Mauthausen fell within the Soviet zone.

THE BEGINNING OF AN OBSESSION

The U.S. War Crimes Office packed up and moved to the city of Linz, in the new American zone. Wiesenthal went with them. He rented a room near the new War Crimes Office. He did not realize that he was just four doors away from the childhood home of Adolf Eichmann.

The name Eichmann did not mean a great deal to Wiesenthal in 1945, although information was already accumulating about the man who would become known as the "architect of the Final Solution."[32] A number of Hungarian Jews said that Eichmann had arranged their deportations to Mauthausen. Captain O'Meara of the American Office of Strategic Services (OSS) told Wiesenthal that Eichmann had been "the head of the [SS] department responsible for Jews."[33]

At the time, Wiesenthal was concentrating on what he called "individual murderers."[34] He wanted to find the people with blood on their hands: those "who humiliated, beat up and shot people dead in front of my own eyes."[35] He had no way of knowing that Eichmann ran the vast bureaucracy that carried out the Nazi extermination plan.

He certainly could not have known that the hunt for this sinister "desk officer" would become his personal obsession. He added the name of Adolf Eichmann to his list of former SS officers wanted for questioning and thought little more about it.

During this period, Wiesenthal visited refugee camps and talked with other survivors. From these interviews, he got more names of Nazi war criminals who should be prosecuted. He also began another list, this one of survivors and their hometowns. He hoped to use it to reunite families that had been torn apart by the war.

On one of those survivor lists, Wiesenthal found the name of a former high school classmate from Buczacz, a Dr. Biener. He wrote to Biener's Cracow address, telling his old friend that Cyla was dead. He asked Biener to find out if her body still lay in the ruins of the house where she had lived as "Irena Kowalska." He had no idea

of the curious set of circumstances his letter would set into motion.

FINDING CYLA

Wiesenthal was haunted by the nameless, faceless end of so many loved ones. For them there were no cemeteries, no headstones, nothing to indicate that they had ever lived. He did not want that to happen to Cyla. He had not been able to save her, but at least he could ensure that she received a proper burial.

Shortly after Biener received Wiesenthal's letter, someone knocked on his door. He answered to find himself looking into the gray-blue eyes of Cyla Wiesenthal. She had come because a mutual friend had told her that Biener might have some information about Simon's "suicide."

Cyla had heard that Simon slashed his wrists while in Gestapo custody. What she had not heard was that he survived. Dr. Biener showed her the letter he had just received. Cyla wrote immediately to Simon.

Their reunion was delayed by red tape and the confusion that had settled over postwar Europe. Because she was in the Soviet zone, Cyla needed special travel documents to cross into American territory.

Simon was laid up with a broken ankle when he received her letter. Fellow survivor Dr. Felix Weisberg volunteered to find Cyla and bring her to safety. The job was anything but routine. Dr. Weisberg ran into a Soviet checkpoint on his way to

Cracow. Fearing arrest because he was traveling with American documents, he destroyed everything but his travel permit. Too late, he realized that he had destroyed Cyla Wiesenthal's address.

Dr. Weisberg found a novel way of dealing with this problem. He posted a notice on the bulletin board at the Jewish Committee offices in Cracow: "Would Cyla Wiesenthal please get in touch with Dr. Felix Weisberg, who will take her to her husband in Linz?"[36]

To Dr. Weisberg's dismay, three women answered the notice. He had not counted on an unpleasant fact of postwar existence: people trapped within the Soviet zone would do almost anything to get out. Two of the women saw a chance and took it. One was the real Cyla Wiesenthal. Never having met Cyla, Weisberg had no way of knowing who was whom.

He talked with all three and chose the one whose story seemed most sincere. He took her with him to Linz. The moment Cyla and Simon saw one another, Dr. Wiesberg knew he had made the right choice.

DREAMS OF THE FUTURE, GHOSTS FROM THE PAST

Even the joy of their reunion could not free the Wiesenthals from the horrors of their past. As childhood sweethearts, they had dreamed of marriage. As newlyweds, they had dreamed of a home, a family, a respected place in the community. As Holocaust survivors, they could dream only of healing.

Part of that healing was having a child. With the years the Nazis had snatched from them, the Wiesenthals feared it was already too late. Both were nearing forty. If they did not have a baby soon, they might not be able to have one at all.

On September 5, 1946, Cyla gave birth to a daughter, Paulinka. The Wiesenthals were overjoyed. She was a symbol of normality and hope in their lives. Cyla wanted to protect the baby from her parents' terrible memories. She feared that Simon's Nazi hunting would make that impossible.

He could not allow himself to forget. For him, survival was more than a fact. It was a call to action. Only by action could he justify his own life and honor the millions who had died. He expressed this sentiment in his own way: "When each of us comes before the six million [Jewish dead], we will be asked what we did with our lives. . . . I will say, 'I did not forget you.'"[37]

While Cyla stayed home with Paulinka, Simon continued his relentless pursuit of war criminals. In the process, he confronted one of his most troubling memories. It started when he saw sunflowers growing in a summer meadow. They brought back uncomfortable memories of the dying SS man who asked his forgiveness.

AN ECHO FROM THE PAST

Two weeks later, he decided to visit the soldier's mother. He had seen her address in the sickroom and taken the trouble to memorize it. When he stood before her house in Stuttgart, he had no idea what to say or how to proceed. He knocked on the door. She answered and invited him inside.

They talked about the war and about Karl. He was a good boy, she said. In the horror of all that had happened, she had one consolation: her son would never have been part of the slaughter. Once more, Wiesenthal faced a choice: tell the truth and take away a grieving mother's one source of comfort, or dodge the issue and leave her memories alone. For reasons that even he could not understand, Wiesenthal chose compassion.

He had not met her son, he said. Someone on a passing hospital train had asked him to find her. It was her son's last wish to send greetings to his mother. The woman accepted this explanation at face value, and thanked Wiesenthal for coming. He never saw her again.

In his book *The Sunflower*, Wiesenthal reflected on his choice: "Perhaps it was a mistake not to have told her the truth. Perhaps her tears might help to wash away some of the misery of the world."[38]

GOING IT ALONE

During 1946 and early 1947, American attitudes toward Nazi war criminals began to change. The men who liberated the camps were being rotated home. Their replacements had never seen the gas chambers and ovens, the stacks of rotting bodies. They were therefore less dedicated to the quest for Nazi criminals and less able to understand Wiesenthal's obsession with justice.

Wiesenthal and his daughter Paulinka.

While many Jews wanted to put the past behind them, Wiesenthal wanted only to remember. Fellow Nazi hunter Tuviah Friedman described Wiesenthal in those days as "an embittered, ruthless, vengeful pursuer of Nazi criminals."[39] His personal quest led to friction with the Americans. An ill-advised joke by one officer brought matters to a head.

The man was trying to convince Wiesenthal to emigrate to the United States. He could make a great career there, the man assured him: "Listen, Simon, in America, the red and green lights regulate traffic and everything else is run by the Jews."[40]

Repentance: A Jewish View

In her response to Simon Wiesenthal's question in The Sunflower, *Jewish studies professor Deborah E. Lipstadt explains repentance as "Judaism's process of saying I'm sorry to those we have wronged."*

"[R]epentance is not a simple thing. . . . First one must ask forgiveness of the [wronged] party. . . . Judaism believes that it is only through human interaction that the victim can best be healed and the wrongdoer most profoundly changed. Making peace with God comes later. By forcing a face-to-face encounter with the [injured] party Jewish tradition teaches that sin is not a generalized . . . act but something quite specific done against a particular person or group of people. . . . After confronting the [wronged] person . . . one turns to God. . . . Then one . . . confesses [sins], expresses shame and regret for having committed this act, and resolves never to act that way again. . . . [The] highest . . . level of the process [is only] achieved when the individual is in the same situation in which he or she originally sinned and chooses not to repeat the act."

The officer was puzzled when Wiesenthal took offense. He was only joking, he said. Wiesenthal knew all too well the dangers of such jokes. They covered an unthinking anti-Semitism that could erupt into genocide, the systematic murder of an entire people.

Then and there, Wiesenthal handed in his resignation. He found thirty survivors who shared his passion for bringing Nazis to justice. Together, they formed the Jewish Historical Documentation Center in Linz, Austria. The group had no money, no headquarters, no sponsorship. All they had was what Wiesenthal called "the right of the victim"[41] and the lists he had made while working for the Americans. From that, they began.

They collected hundreds of statements from survivors, adding to the lists as they went along. They kept lists of criminals, victims, witnesses. By 1947, the Documentation Center had a tiny office in Linz, and a growing reputation all over the world. Testimonies of victims and witnesses began coming in the mail. Wiesenthal and his people checked every one and incorporated the information into their files.

The Three Rabbis

In his journey from concentration camp inmate to Nazi hunter, Wiesenthal experienced several turning points. The sunflowers, the dying soldier, the unthinking joke by an American officer were all turning points. So was a strange request from three rabbis. They had heard that a vast library of Jewish religious books existed in a castle near the town of Villach. They wanted Wiesenthal to help them save those books.

The Nazis had carefully collected these treasures and stored them. After the war, which they expected to win, they planned to open museums and libraries. These new institutions would display the artifacts of an extinct culture: European Jewry. The projected victory, of course, did not happen, and so it fell to the trio of rabbis to save the collection.

Saving books was not part of Wiesenthal's mission, but the pleas of the rabbis moved him. He went with them to the castle. It was packed top to bottom with Bibles, prayer books, Talmuds (Jewish religious writings), and other books from all over Europe. The rabbis started looking through the stacks. They handled each book reverently. In their eyes, these books were like living things, infinitely precious and beloved.

The youngest of the three rabbis found a prayer book that looked oddly familiar. When he opened it, he gasped and passed out on the floor. When he regained consciousness, he broke into tears. It was his own prayer book. His

Allied troops view a jumbled mass of Dachau concentration camp victims.

COLLECTIVE RESPONSIBILITY: A PSYCHIATRIST'S VIEW

Dr. Viktor Frankl was a distinguished psychiatrist in Vienna. He survived three years of imprisonment in Nazi concentration camps, including Auschwitz and Dachau. He shares Simon Wiesenthal's opposition to collective guilt, as he explains in his book Man's Search for Meaning.

"As for the concept of collective guilt, I personally think that it is totally unjustified to hold one person responsible for the behavior of another person or [group] of persons. Since the end of World War II, I have not become weary of publicly arguing against the collective guilt concept. Sometimes . . . it takes a lot of . . . [teaching] to detach people from their superstitions. An American woman once confronted me with the reproach, 'How can you still write some of your books in German, Adolf Hitler's language?' In response, I asked her if she had knives in her kitchen, and when she answered that she did, I acted . . . shocked, exclaiming, 'How can you still use knives after so many killers have used them to stab and murder their victims?' She stopped objecting to my writing books in German."

sister had written a last message inside it: "Whoever will find this prayer book, give it to my beloved brother, Rabbi Joshua Zeitman. The murderers are in our village. They are in the next home. . . . Please don't forget us! And don't forget our murderers!"[42]

"Please don't forget." In the car on the way back home, Wiesenthal thought about those words. They were not just the last thoughts of a woman who was about to die. They were a call to action. He vowed to answer that call: "[T]his is what drives me—and always will."[43]

4 Occupation: Nazi Hunter

Simon Wiesenthal was a tireless investigator. Tracking Nazi criminals was only part of his self-appointed mission. He also looked for Nazis who behaved honorably and civilian collaborators who did not. Real justice demanded that each person be judged by his or her deeds. Crimes should be punished and decency acknowledged. To do otherwise would dishonor the dead.

Not everyone agreed with Wiesenthal. Some thought all Nazis bore part of the guilt for the Holocaust. Some went even farther and wanted to condemn all Germans. This is the idea of collective guilt. Wiesenthal rejected it out of hand.

THE STRANGE CASE
OF DR. WASYL STRONCICKIJ

Next door to the Documentation Center offices, a doctor named Wasyl Stroncickij ran an organization for Ukrainian refugees. He was a camp survivor who had spent three and a half years in Auschwitz and Mauthausen.

Wiesenthal was immediately interested. Ukrainian camp survivors were a rarity. Ukrainian collaborators were not. Units of Ukrainian police routinely assisted in the roundup and execution of Jews. This Ukrainian did not fit the profile. Wiesenthal sensed a story, possibly a heroic one.

Then he interviewed Adolf and Antoine Weiler. The Jewish couple came from Stroncickij's hometown. About fifteen hundred Jews had lived there before the Nazis came. Only a handful survived. The rest were rounded up like cattle and systematically slaughtered. The roundups were conducted by "a certain Dr. Stroncickij, one of the worst Jew-baiters."[44] Stroncickij served as mayor of the town, first under the Soviets and later under the Nazis. He willingly ordered the Ukrainian guards to kill Jews.

Stroncickij's men took their Jewish prisoners into the forest and made them dig huge trenches. Then they lined everyone up in front of these freshly dug trenches and gunned them down. "It was said that when he came back from the wood Stroncickij was spattered all over with blood,"[45] the Weilers concluded.

Stroncickij was not a common name. To have more than one "Dr. Wasyl Stroncickij"

CRIMES AGAINST HUMANITY

The international tribunal at Nuremberg had an awesome task: to dispense justice for some of the most horrifying crimes in history. In Pursuit of Justice: Examining the Evidence of the Holocaust, *edited by Kevin Mahoney, explains the nature of the charges.*

"According to its Charter, the International Military Tribunal had legal [authority] to try individuals accused of *(a) crimes against peace:* the planning, preparation . . . or waging of a war of aggression or in violation of international treaties . . . .*(b) war crimes:* violations . . . such as . . . ill-treatment of prisoners, killing of hostages, using civilians as slave labor, and wanton destruction not justified by military necessity; *(c) crimes against humanity:* atrocities such as murder, extermination, deportation of civilian populations, and persecutions on political, racial, or religious grounds; *(d) conspiracy to commit these crimes. . . .*

On October 18, 1945, less than half a year after the war ended, twenty-four major Nazi war criminals were indicted for their crimes. Hitler and some of his leading henchmen, such as Reich Leader of the SS and Chief of the German Police Heinrich Himmler and Propaganda Minister Joseph Goebbels, were absent—they had all committed suicide when they saw the war was lost. The head of Hitler's Nazi Party Chancellery and his private secretary, Martin Bormann, had disappeared and was to be tried *in absentia.* Leader of the German Labor Front Robert Ley took his own life after the indictment was served upon him. Hermann Göring, Hitler's second in command and a major planner of the Nazi policies of persecution and extermination, sat morosely at the head of the dock. The evidence against him was overwhelming, but he too was to cheat the hangman by swallowing a cyanide capsule after being convicted on all counts on October 1, 1946."

Captured Nazi war criminals are put on trial for their crimes.

in the same small town was almost impossible. Somehow, this man had gone from killer to victim. How could such a thing have happened?

The answer was nothing short of amazing. The Nazi town commander was an Austrian, *Oberleutnant* Kroupa. He was in charge of a huge store of captured weapons. Jewish forced laborers performed much of the work of maintaining and repairing the weaponry. Kroupa saw to it that the workers received enough food and medical attention. When he learned that SS and Ukrainian guards were mistreating the workers, he ordered an immediate halt to this practice.

Stroncickij was furious. He denounced Kroupa to his superiors for "pro-Jewish" attitudes. The commander's defense was both forthright and clever. He argued that the work of sorting and reconditioning weapons required trained people. Keeping the Jewish workers healthy was therefore necessary to the German war effort.

The argument worked and Kroupa was acquitted, or found not guilty. He immediately dealt with Stroncickij. He called the Ukrainian to his office, then ripped insignia and buttons from his own uniform and yelled for his orderly. When the startled soldier arrived, Kroupa claimed that Stroncickij had assaulted him, and also "insulted Germany and the führer."[46]

The Ukrainian ended up in a concentration camp, and Kroupa went ahead with his duties. The story the Weilers told had the ring of truth, and Wiesenthal was able to verify most of it.

In spite of his strong evidence against Stroncickij, the Americans refused to place the man on trial. He was an intelligence source, they said. His information had proved valuable in the growing conflict with the Soviets.

Stroncickij was never prosecuted for his crimes, nor was Kroupa rewarded for his decency. Wiesenthal learned that the *Oberleutnant* was in a Soviet prisoner-of-war camp. He wrote a letter explaining Kroupa's actions to the Soviets and asking for leniency. He never received a reply, nor did he learn the fate of this man who had protected his Jewish workers.

The injustice of the situation stung Wiesenthal, but it did not surprise him. He was learning a hard truth: in relation to the Holocaust, complete justice did not exist. Nowhere was this more apparent than in dealing with Jews who had been forced to govern the ghettos for their Nazi overlords.

WIESENTHAL'S LAW

In each ghetto the Nazis appointed a Jewish council to run day-to-day operations and a Jewish police unit to enforce their rulings. Even the most principled of these officials had to do some terrible things. When the Nazis wanted slave laborers, the council had to deliver them. When they wanted to reduce the ghetto population, the Jewish police had to fill the transports. The deportees went to almost certain death in the camps.

Because of the work they were forced to do, Wiesenthal regarded all Jewish officials as suspect. Some had behaved as honorably as they could under the circumstances.

Others did not. They brutalized fellow Jews, took payoffs and bribes, even informed on Jews who were disobeying Nazi regulations.

It was not possible to know the record of every Jewish council member and policeman. Wiesenthal therefore established a policy that became known as "Wiesenthal's Law." Anyone who "had a function of authority in the Nazi period could not have a function in postwar Jewish life."[47] The American authorities went along with this "law" in order to protect the survivors.

INVESTIGATING
A JEWISH POLICEMAN

One collaborator who earned Wiesenthal's wrath was a man named David Zimet (also spelled Zimmet). A Jewish

The Jewish Council of Lublin in 1939.

policeman in the ghetto of Tarnów, Zimet worked closely with the Gestapo. He brutalized his fellow Jews so terribly that he was perhaps the most hated man in the ghetto. Again and again, survivors from Tarnów told of the indignities they had suffered at his hands.

Wiesenthal launched a full investigation. When Zimet learned of this, he flew into a rage and attacked the Nazi hunter with a knife. Wiesenthal barely escaped with his life. For this attack, Zimet was placed under arrest. After four weeks in jail, the authorities released him to give testimony at war crimes trials. Zimet made his court appearance and then disappeared.

Years later, Wiesenthal found him living in Canada. He immediately contacted Canadian authorities. Because Zimet was Jewish, the government handed his case over to the Canadian Jewish Committee. The committee took no action for fear that the publicity would reflect poorly upon the entire Jewish community.

Simon Wiesenthal did not agree. To him, a war criminal was a war criminal. Ignoring those who happened to be Jewish was wrong. It was also bad politics. "If everybody could see that we are not looking only for Germans and Ukrainians, but even for our own Jewish criminals, then we would have much less opposition,"[48] he told Alan Levy.

NAZIS ON TRIAL
AND ON THE RUN

In October 1945, an international tribunal indicted, or charged, twenty-four Nazi leaders with crimes against humanity. The trials began in November at Nuremberg, Germany.

Several other trials followed: of Nazi doctors who conducted cruel experiments on prisoners, of ghetto and camp commanders, of SS men who served on the murder squads that killed thousands of Russian Jews.

Wiesenthal spent some time at these trials, but he was neither a prosecutor nor a frequent observer. Mostly he took advantage of the vast archives the Allies had assembled. He studied them for evidence that might be used in future trials.

Some people who knew Wiesenthal were surprised that he did not take a more active interest in the proceedings. His reason for this was simple: He was not so much interested in the Nazis on trial as he was in the ones that got away. Some of the worst criminals were slipping through the hands of the authorities.

By late 1947, Wiesenthal was beginning to realize that these escapes were carefully planned. A secret organization was at work, providing safe houses, false papers, and transportation to Nazis fleeing prosecution. The first clue to this organization came through an Austrian investigation of black-market activities. Black marketeers made a fortune by selling scarce and illegally obtained goods at high prices.

A man named Theodor Soucek was using black-market profits to smuggle Nazi war criminals out of the country. As it turned out, Soucek's operation was part of a much larger conspiracy: the Organization of Former SS Members (with German initials ODESSA).

A Jewish policeman (center) reports the crimes of a woman to a German officer.

TRACKING ODESSA

The official purpose of ODESSA was to render humanitarian aid to German prisoners of war. Its actual purpose was more sinister.

ODESSA smuggled Nazi war criminals to safe havens in Arab countries, Spain, and South America. It gave them new names, new occupations, new personal histories. It also gave many of them a new mission.

Even before the war ended, Nazi industrialists and government leaders had been transferring funds to dozens of small accounts. Some of these accounts were in foreign countries. They were established in the names of dummy corporations or hidden in the accounts of low-ranking officers who were not likely to be investigated. This money was supposed to finance a rebirth of the empire.

Through painstaking checking and cross-checking, Wiesenthal discovered the main escape routes. They were cleverly designed. Even knowing the starting and ending points was not enough to break the organization. ODESSA passed fugitives through a changing network of staging posts, moving them from link to link and finally out of the country. Any kind of transport might be used.

For example, some of the trucks that hauled the American army newspaper, *Stars and Stripes*, carried fugitives as well. The drivers were German civilians, employed by the U.S. Army but actually working for ODESSA. The trucks were rarely searched. At most, a military policeman might take a quick look inside. He would see only bundles of newspapers, not the fugitives crouched behind those bundles.

Wiesenthal reported this to American intelligence. His information led to the arrest of one driver and the end of that particular route. Unfortunately, it did not lead to the end of ODESSA. The organiza-

Hans Frank (standing) speaking at the Nuremberg trials.

THE EXECUTION SQUADS

"I went out to the woods alone. The [army] had already dug a grave. The children were brought along in a tractor. I had nothing to do with this technical procedure. The Ukrainians were standing round trembling. The children were taken down from the tractor. They were lined up along the top of the grave and shot so that they fell into it. The Ukrainians did not aim at any particular part of the body. They fell into the grave. The wailing was indescribable. I shall never forget the scene throughout my life. I find it very hard to bear. I particularly remember a small fair-haired girl who took me by the hand. She too was shot later. . . . The execution must have taken place in the afternoon at about 3:30 or 4:00. . . . Many children were hit four or five times before they died."

tion had many other routes that remained secure. It also had an estimated 1 billion dollars scattered in banks and businesses all over the world.

Neither Simon Wiesenthal nor anyone else could stamp out ODESSA. They could only hunt escaping criminals one by one, plugging up ODESSA escape hatches whenever and wherever they found them.

THE HUNT FOR ADOLF EICHMANN

While Wiesenthal investigated ODESSA, he acquired more information on Adolf Eichmann. The more he learned, the more certain he became that Eichmann was a criminal of the first order. For Wiesenthal, he became an obsession. It was not only the man's crimes that stunned Wiesenthal; it was his apparent normality.

War criminals were supposed to be evil and sadistic, people who enjoyed cruelty. Adolf Eichmann did not fit the profile. He did not kill people with his bare hands, torture them, or experiment upon them. He loved his family, got along with his neighbors, and did his work to the best of his ability.

One survivor recalled his shock upon seeing Eichmann for the first time. He told a reporter for the *Cleveland Jewish News* that he had "expected . . . to see a big, brutal

German type. 'Instead, I found a rat, a mouse, with frightened eyes.' This . . . wisp of a man with a receding hairline and a permanent sneer on his thin face . . . was placed in charge of the 'Jewish question.'"[49]

As head of Jewish Affairs, Eichmann was directly responsible for carrying out the "Final Solution," the name the Nazis gave to the extermination of European Jews. He arranged mass deportations, kept the death camps running, and prided himself on the efficiency of the extermination program.

The Eichmann hunt took fifteen years and spanned two continents. For Wiesenthal, it began in earnest after he moved to Linz. Until then, "Eichmann" had been only one name among the many on his list of war criminals. Then he discovered that an elderly couple named Eichmann lived just a few doors down from him. They had a son named Adolf, who had been a high-ranking officer in the SS. At Wiesenthal's urging, the OSS searched the family home and questioned Eichmann's parents.

The search turned up nothing. The elder Eichmanns claimed that they did not know the whereabouts of their son. When they last heard of him, he was in Prague, and they supposed he had been taken prisoner by the Russians.

A few weeks later, Wiesenthal got a tip that Adolf Eichmann was hiding in the village of Altaussee, about a hundred miles from Linz. The informant even gave an address: number 8, Fischerndorf Street.

Concentration camp personnel display canisters of Zyklon B, which was used to gas inmates.

On the strength of this information, the Austrian police went to search the house. Unfortunately, they got the wrong address. Instead of going to number 8, they went to number 38. The mistake allowed Eichmann time to get away.

His wife and children did live at number 8, but Veronika Liebl Eichmann denied that Adolf had ever been there. She claimed that she had divorced her husband in 1945 and had not seen him since. Wiesenthal did not believe her, so he arranged to have the family watched.

PUTTING A FACE ON EVIL

At this point, none of the Nazi hunters would have known Eichmann by sight. Neither his wife nor his parents admitted to having a photo. Wiesenthal explains:

> [Eichmann's] father [said] that, as a matter of principle, Adolf had refused to be photographed. At first we didn't believe that, but it turned out to be the truth. Eichmann was evidently aware that he was doing something that might . . . expose him to prosecution.[50]

Wiesenthal investigated relatives, associates, schoolmates, and friends of Eichmann. None of them had a photo. Finally, Eichmann investigator Manus Diamant found a picture in the scrapbook of one of Eichmann's former girlfriends. As Wiesenthal put it, "Now our wanted man had a face."[51]

In 1947, Veronika Eichmann petitioned to have her husband declared dead.

Nazi war criminal Adolf Eichmann.

Hundreds of German women whose husbands never returned from the war were making these petitions. Some needed an official death certificate in order to receive survivor benefits for themselves and their children. Others needed it in order to remarry.

Wiesenthal thought Veronika Eichmann had a different reason. If her husband was officially dead, the Nazi hunters would cross his name off their lists. He could build a new life without fear of capture. Simon Wiesenthal was determined that this should not happen.

He checked Mrs. Eichmann's petition. It cited the testimony of a certain "Karl

Lucas." Lucas stated under oath that he saw Adolf Eichmann killed in Prague, Czechoslovakia, on April 30, 1945. Wiesenthal contacted his sources in Prague, asking them to check the story.

They found that Karl Lucas was Veronika Eichmann's brother-in-law. On the strength of this evidence, the court turned down her petition. Wiesenthal called this "my most important contribution to the Eichmann case."[52]

THE GHOST OF MARTIN BORMANN

The same dogged determination that kept the Eichmann case alive could sometimes lead Wiesenthal in wrong directions. His hunt for Hitler's chief deputy, Martin Bormann, was a case in point. When Russian troops conquered Berlin, they found no trace of Bormann. Some thought he died in the bunker (underground shelter) with other top Nazis. Others believed he got away.

Wiesenthal cast his lot with the second group. He chose to believe that Bormann was alive. Faking death was a favorite means of escape for many Nazis. Wiesenthal knew this. He also knew that Holocaust survivors, himself included, needed to believe that their tormentors were alive

THE MYSTERY OF MARTIN BORMANN

After World War II, Martin Bormann became an almost mythic figure. His career in the Nazi party put him close to Hitler and made him part of the ruling elite, as explained by Ralph Haswell Lutz in Colliers Encyclopedia.

"[Martin Bormann] . . . joined the Nazi Party in 1925. [I]n 1930 he was placed in charge of the 'special fund' for political propaganda, and in 1933 became commander of the party's . . . headquarters at Munich. He checked the list of party members to be liquidated in the 1934 purge and the list of army officers to be retired in 1938. In the Nazi secret police Bormann was chief of the Gestapo section, charged with the surveillance of party leaders. . . . He replaced [Rudolf] Hess in 1941 as Deputy Führer, and after Hitler and [SS chief Heinrich] Himmler was the most powerful man in Nazi Germany. . . . As the Russians advanced on Berlin, Bormann's voice was heard over the radio from Hitler's headquarters broadcasting party orders and proclamations. The Russians failed to find him when they captured the chancellery. . . . In 1973 a West German court certified that a skeleton found at a Berlin construction site was that of Bormann. He had committed suicide on May 2, 1945."

and would one day be brought to justice. Finding a dead criminal was not enough. Wiesenthal wrote, "the thought that a mass murderer simply lives on after the war, that he grows old and eventually passes away peacefully, is intolerable."[53]

This attitude was partly responsible for the long postwar "career" of Martin Bormann. Before it was established that Bormann killed himself in 1945, a vast body of legend built up around him.

THE END OF A LEGEND

There were Bormann sightings all over the world, many from credible informants. Dozens of men who had the misfortune to resemble Bormann were arrested and held until they could prove their identities. Bormann stories flooded the pages of newspapers and magazines. Bogus journalists even sold "exclusive interviews" with him. In the general Bormann hysteria, Wiesenthal collected two thousand pages of information on the deputy führer's supposed whereabouts and activities.

In 1973, the Frankfurt prosecutor's office found and identified Bormann's remains. Wiesenthal never liked giving up a hunt. He was even less enthusiastic about admitting that he was wrong. Still, the evidence was solid; he could not refute it. He accepted the prosecutor's findings and put the Bormann information into his inactive file.

Hitler's chief deputy Martin Bormann escaped the postwar Nazi hunt by killing himself.

In a sense, the Bormann case was a triumph for Wiesenthal. Many people knew little or nothing about the police reports. They simply believed that Bormann was dead because Wiesenthal said he was. In the same way, they had believed Eichmann was alive because Wiesenthal never gave up the hunt. In matters of Nazi war crimes, the name of Simon Wiesenthal had become its own kind of proof.

5 In the Shadow of the Holocaust

In the early 1950s, postwar Europe was undergoing important changes. People on both sides wanted to put the war behind them and get on with their lives. The displaced persons camps, temporary shelters for war victims, emptied as Holocaust survivors found new homes. Some emigrated to the United States, Canada, or South America. Some returned to their former homes in Europe. Some went to Israel, which had been newly established by the United Nations in May 1948.

The young Jews who had worked at Wiesenthal's Documentation Center also began to leave. They gave up the Nazi hunt for a more personal dream: the chance for a normal life. For Simon Wiesenthal, it was a time of crisis. He sensed that he had come to another turning point. He faced choices that would shape the rest of his life.

THE TIME BETWEEN

In 1953, Wiesenthal had reached a stalemate in the Eichmann investigation. He simply did not have the resources to pursue the leads he had gathered. Hoping to get financial help, he contacted Dr. Nahum Goldmann of the World Jewish Congress (WJC) in New York.

Dr. Goldmann did not respond. Wiesenthal later learned the reason for this silence: the WJC would not support independent projects. The only way he could get funding was to work within the organization—something Wiesenthal refused to do.

In 1955, he closed the Linz Documentation Center. He sent his files to Yad Vashem, the Holocaust memorial and study center in Israel. According to Hella Pick, the Linz archive "weighs several

Jews prepare to leave Germany for Israel.

hundred kilos, contains material on 365 war criminals, and takes up ten meters [over thirty-two feet] of shelving at Yad Vashem."[54] The only file not included in that huge shipment was the one that haunted him more than any other: the Eichmann investigation.

The closing of the center left Wiesenthal at loose ends. Without his self-appointed task, life no longer seemed to have purpose. Though his heart was not in it, Wiesenthal accepted a position with the Organization for Rehabilitation and Training (ORT), a Jewish vocational training organization.

His first job was to set up classes in Linz and the surrounding area. His duties expanded after the Hungarian uprising of 1956 brought floods of Jewish refugees into Austria. He traveled the country to set up new centers.

AN UNEXPECTED CHALLENGE

In 1958, a group of Austrian teenagers pulled him back into the Nazi hunting business. Wiesenthal overheard them in a coffeehouse discussing a performance of the play *The Diary of Anne Frank*. Another group of young people had picketed the theater, carrying signs that said the diary was a fraud, that Anne Frank had never existed.

Such claims could be the beginning of the forgetfulness Wiesenthal feared. Already the Holocaust was fading into the background of history. The Documentation Center was closed, the Nuremberg trials long completed. Young people in particular had begun to doubt the Holo-

The personal memoirs of Anne Frank were an indisputable account of Nazi brutality that instantly became one of the bestselling biographies of all time.

caust had ever happened. Perhaps Jews were persecuted along the way; perhaps some of them died. But six million? That had to be an exaggeration.

To those who wanted to deny the Holocaust, Anne Frank's diary was a dangerous thing. It had a strange power to move anyone who read it. Young people in particular identified with Anne's experiences. Her words brought the Holocaust to life for them.

Wiesenthal struck up a conversation with the boys in the coffeehouse. He pointed out that Anne's father, Otto, was still alive. So were many of the people who knew the family during their years in hiding. All these people had testified about Anne and the diary.

The boys were not impressed. Maybe the witnesses had reason to lie, they said. Maybe Otto Frank had created the diary himself. Wiesenthal asked what it would take to convince them that Anne's diary was genuine. Suppose he found the Gestapo man who arrested Anne and her family at their hideout in Amsterdam? Would that be proof enough?

Yes, said one of the boys—if the man admitted his actions. To most anyone besides Simon Wiesenthal, the task of finding this man would have seemed impossible. There was no arrest report to read, no archive to explore. The search would take him more than five years.

TRACING HALF A NAME

All he had to start with was half a name: "Silver" or "Silber." One of Otto Frank's employees remembered him as the SS man who took the Franks into custody. Wiesenthal checked out seven "Silbernagels" and three "Silvertalers" with no success. Finally, he got hold of a Gestapo telephone directory. He turned to the listing for Department IV, B4; the unit that had been responsible for arresting Jews. One name fairly jumped off the page: "Silberbauer."

Most of the men in the Jewish department had been policemen in civilian life. Many of them went back to their jobs after the war. Wiesenthal called a friend in the Austrian Ministry of the Interior and announced that he had found the man who arrested Anne Frank: an Austrian policeman named Silberbauer.

Since there were at least six Silberbauers on the force in Vienna alone, the ministry friend saw little hope of success, but he promised to investigate. On October 15, 1963, Wiesenthal inquired about developments in the Silberbauer matter.

There had been none, the official told him. The matter was still under investigation. Several weeks later, Wiesenthal learned that this was not true. Inspector Karl Silberbauer of the Vienna police force had been suspended from duty on October 4, due to his part in the Anne Frank case.

The Austrian authorities had intended to keep the matter quiet. Silberbauer was so outraged over his suspension that he revealed his secret to a fellow officer. From there, the story made its way to the press.

The ministry official was embarrassed to be caught in a lie, Silberbauer was branded by his own words, and Simon Wiesenthal had accomplished the impossible. He often wondered about the boy whose challenge had triggered the investigation. Did he read the papers? Did the exposure of Silberbauer change his mind about Anne Frank? There was no way to know. Wiesenthal never saw him again.

Amid all the furor there was new interest in Wiesenthal and his work. He had tracked Eichmann all those years, keeping the case alive when others might have given up the hunt. A friend in the publishing industry asked Wiesenthal to write a book about his long search. The 1961 German book, *Ich Jagte Eichmann* (I Hunted Eichmann), was the result. It became an instant best-seller in Germany and Austria.

A NOTE OF DISCORD

All this attention to Wiesenthal angered Israeli agent Isser Harel, the man responsible for the capture of Adolf Eichmann. After Eichmann was traced to Argentina, it was Harel who led the daring mission that brought him to justice In May 1960, Harel's team captured Eichmann and spirited him out of the country.

They did not go through official channels for fear that the Argentinean authorities would refuse to extradite, or deliver their prisoner to Israeli authorities. Because of this and other secret matters, the Israeli government ordered Harel to keep silent about his operation.

Eichmann was tried in Jerusalem, found guilty, and hanged on May 31, 1962. Still Harel did not speak. Resentment simmered as his deed went unrecognized by all but a select few.

Harel never ceased to blame Wiesenthal for grabbing all the glory. When his operation was finally declassified, he wrote his own book on Eichmann: *The House on Garibaldi Street* (referring to Eichmann's residence in Buenos Aires) was published in 1975. Harel did not even mention Simon Wiesenthal. Later, he told a reporter for the *Jerusalem Post* that the information Wiesenthal had supplied over the years was "utterly worthless."[55]

Wiesenthal did not take kindly to this sort of criticism. He never claimed to be "a Jewish James Bond,"[56] chasing war criminals through exotic locales. He never claimed to have participated in the final capture of Eichmann. Still, he believed that his contribution was significant.

It was his pursuit that kept the case alive. It was his protest that prevented Veronika Eichmann from having her divorced husband declared dead. In Wiesenthal's mind, this was enough to ensure him a place in the long and strange history of the Eichmann hunt.

THE EVILDOERS

The Adolf Eichmann trial forced survivors to recall things they would rather forget. The reactions were powerful, painful, and often unexpected, as writer Stephen Lutz explains in his article, "People Must Acknowledge Their Tendencies to Do Evil."

"Walking into the courtroom, [Holocaust survivor Yehiel] Dinur saw Eichmann in person for the first time. He stopped and began to sob uncontrollably. He then collapsed. Why this response? Was it years of fear, or hatred or terrible memories all coming to the surface? This is Dinur's explanation: '. . . I was afraid about myself. . . . I saw that I am capable to do this. I am . . . exactly like he.'

Dinur was scared precisely because Eichmann was not a monster. Instead, Eichmann was frighteningly normal. Dinur understood that the most terrifying thing about Adolf Eichmann was that he was just like the rest of us."

The Architect of the "Final Solution"

The trial of Adolf Eichmann in 1961 revealed the full horror of the Holocaust and the nature of the man himself, who could make chilling statements about his "task." An article in the Cleveland Jewish News *quotes some revealing statements Eichmann made at his trial.*

"'The work I've done willingly and I felt at home in it,' [Eichmann] wrote of his initial efforts in Austria. Later, as expulsion gave way to wholesale murder and gassing of Jews, Eichmann [wrote to his superiors] 'I am delighted to inform you that the children's transports [consisting of 1,000 children each] can be moved from Drancy [a transit station in France] to Auschwitz.'

When the commandant of Auschwitz noted in his memoirs that he once told Eichmann his knees got 'wobbly' when he killed 1,000 children in a day, the architect of the 'Final Solution' reassured him. It was more important to kill children than old people, Eichmann told the commandant, since that would prevent having any 'avengers' later."

Polish children were numbered and photographed upon arrival at a concentration camp.

Adolf Eichmann was finally brought to trial for his crimes and was executed on May 31, 1967.

MOVING ON

After Eichmann, Cyla Wiesenthal may well have hoped that her husband would finally come to terms with the past. The hunt was over. Eichmann was on trial. Perhaps now they could begin to live a more normal life.

Cyla wanted to move to Israel. There, the family would be safe and Simon could find rewarding work. He did not see it that way. With the trial renewing public interest in Nazi war crimes, it was not time to quit. It was time to renew the hunt. Instead of going to Israel, he chose to move to Vienna. There in Austria's capital, he could start again.

Cyla was horrified. For her, Austria was a terrifying place. Not only was it full of painful memories, it was still a hotbed of anti-Semitism. Simon's Nazi hunting activities had made the whole family a special target of this unthinking hatred.

There were still many Austrians trying to hide their Nazi pasts. Wiesenthal's private crusade scared them. They considered him an obsessed avenger, out to get anyone who once wore a German uniform. Wiesenthal's insistence that he was only after proven war criminals did not change their minds. Almost daily, he received hate mail and death threats.

Simon was resolved to live with the danger. Cyla was not. One night in 1963, a phone call tore her world apart. An anonymous voice told her that Paulinka, their daughter, would be killed if Simon continued his Nazi hunting activities.

Simon was away from home at the time. He returned to find his wife tearful and distraught. For days, she could not think about anything but that voice on the phone. Once more, she begged her husband to take the family to Israel.

A Painful Choice

Even to please Cyla, Wiesenthal could not see himself making a career in ORT or a life in Israel. His place was in Austria, where former Nazis were finding their way into prominent positions. There he could make a difference. There he could pursue the chief goals of his life: justice for the criminals, remembrance for the victims.

Once more, Wiesenthal told his wife that he had to stay in Vienna. Perhaps it would be best if she and Paulinka moved to Israel without him. Cyla refused. As much as she wanted to get away from the danger and the memories, she would not leave her husband to do it.

That was an important decision for both the Wiesenthals. It meant that Cyla was resigned to living in the shadow of the Holocaust. Simon's mission would not allow them to do anything else.

Establishing a Documentation Center in Vienna was not an easy task. With no money and no organization behind him, Wiesenthal had to do his own fundraising. Somehow, he managed to get together enough money to open an office and begin his research. In time, his bulging files came to include twenty-two thousand suspects.

Obviously, he could not follow every lead. He publicized the list of suspects through the newsletters he sent to supporters and the hundreds of files he sent to the appropriate authorities in the countries where his suspects lived. He knew that most of these people would never be captured, let alone tried and convicted. Still, he saw a value in the list. If fugitives could not feel safe, if they were constantly looking over their shoulders for fear of being recognized, that too was a kind of punishment. As Wiesenthal's biographer wrote, "it was better than allowing them a peaceful old age."[57]

Simon Wiesenthal investigating escaped Nazi war criminals.

Wiesenthal focused his attention on those he considered the worst criminals. Among his targets were Franz Stangl, commandant of the Treblinka extermination camp; Dr. Josef Mengele, the Auschwitz doctor who performed brutal medical experiments on helpless prisoners; and Hermine Braunsteiner, the sadistic guard in the women's barracks at the Majdanek camp.

THE DEATH CAMP COMMANDANT: FRANZ STANGL

In Wiesenthal's view, Franz Stangl was almost in a league with Eichmann. Like Eichmann, he did not kill with his own hands. He gave the orders and let others do the work. He made Treblinka into an efficient factory that mass-produced death.

Wiesenthal first encountered Stangl's name in 1948. He was looking through a list of SS officers who had received decorations when a penciled note caught his eye: "Top secret—for psychological stress."[58]

This was the code the Nazis used to avoid mentioning gruesome details in their honors list. Wiesenthal knew that the "psychological stress" came from ordering and witnessing unspeakable horrors. Franz Stangl had worked at the extermination camps. Wiesenthal flagged the name for further investigation.

Stangl's murderous career started at Schloss Hartheim. This was one of the so-called euthanasia, or mercy killing, centers. The euthanasia program did not involve the mass murder of whole peo-

Franz Paul Stangl, commandant of the Treblinka death camp, was wanted for sending thousands of Jews to their deaths.

ples. It was aimed at the physically and mentally handicapped, people the Nazis classed as "life unworthy of life."[59]

The euthanasia program began in October 1939 and officially ended in August 1941. During that time, the Nazis killed at least seventy thousand people. They also learned a great deal about killing: how to do it quickly and efficiently. Many of the euthanasia center workers were later transferred to death camps, where they could put this knowledge to work.

Franz Stangl went from Schloss Hartheim to the Sobibor death camp, and finally to

Treblinka, where he served as commandant. At Treblinka alone, Stangl personally oversaw the killing of some seventy to eighty thousand human beings.

As often happened in Wiesenthal's work, he discovered the importance of Stangl almost by accident. In a talk about the euthanasia centers, he happened to mention the name of Franz Stangl. Some time later, "an evil-looking, unkempt type called on me at my office."[60] The man claimed to be a former member of the Gestapo—and he had information to sell, information about Franz Stangl.

FRANZ STANGL'S INFERNO

Journalist Gitta Sereny interviewed Franz Stangl in prison. The man who had sent thousands to their deaths admitted that he "got used to" the killing. In her article "Colloquy with a Conscience," Sereny records her dialogue with Stangl.

"[Sereny:] *'Would it be true to say that you finally felt they [the prisoners] weren't really human beings?'*
'When I was on a trip once, years later in Brazil,' he said, his face deeply concentrated, and obviously reliving this experience, 'my train stopped next to a slaughterhouse. The cattle in the pens, hearing the noise of the train, trotted up to the fence and stared at the train. They were very close to my window, one crowding the other, looking at me through that fence. I thought then "look at this; this reminds me of Poland"; that's just how the people looked, trustingly, just before they went into the tins. . . .'
[Sereny:] *'You said "tins," I interrupted. What do you mean?'*
But he went on without hearing or answering me.
'. . . I couldn't eat tinned meat after that. Those eyes . . . which looked at me . . . not knowing that in no time at all they'd be dead.' He paused. His face was drawn. At this moment he looked old and worn and real—it was his moment of truth.
[Sereny:] *'So you didn't feel they were human beings?'*
'Chattels,' he said tonelessly, 'they were chattels [property].' He raised and dropped a hand in a gesture of despair. Both our voices had dropped. It was one of the few times in those weeks of talks that he made no effort to cloak his despair, and his hopeless grief allowed a moment of sympathy."

Stangl (left) and his lawyers during his 1970 trial.

Wiesenthal agreed to pay the man only if his information led to the arrest of Franz Stangl. After some attempts at bargaining, the man agreed to Wiesenthal's terms. Stangl was working at a Volkswagen plant in Brazil, the informant said. He did not know where Stangl lived, or what name he was using.

By following this tip, Wiesenthal learned that Stangl had entered Brazil in 1951. He had not even bothered to take a different name. Wiesenthal wanted to go to Brazil and take personal charge of the investigation, but he could not raise the money for the trip.

He settled for his usual procedures: press conferences, requests for evidence from governments, testimonies from survivors, and talks with legal authorities. He succeeded in convincing both Germany and Austria to issue warrants for Stangl. The next step was more difficult. He had to convince the Brazilian authorities to arrest and extradite Franz Stangl.

That part of the process took three years. Not until June 8, 1967, did the Brazilian Supreme Court agree to send Stangl to West Germany. It was the first time Brazil had extradited any accused Nazi criminal.

On December 22, 1970, a West German court sentenced Franz Stangl to life in prison. He died in prison less than a year later, of natural causes. Simon Wiesenthal regarded the Stangl case as one of his most successful: "If I have done nothing else in my life but bring this wicked man to trial, I will not have lived in vain,"[61] he told one biographer.

THE ANGEL OF DEATH: DR. JOSEF MENGELE

In the annals of Nazi war criminals, Josef Mengele achieved a near mythic status. To many people, he was more demon

MENGELE ON THE RAMP

At Auschwitz, arriving prisoners went through a process of "selection." An SS doctor looked over the new arrivals and decided on the spot who would live and who would die. Most doctors were straightforward and "professional" during these selections. Some openly disliked the duty. Dr. Josef Mengele enjoyed it. In his book The Nazi Doctors, *Robert Jay Lifton describes how Mengele behaved during selections.*

"Former inmates describe him as an elegant figure on the ramp—handsome, well groomed, extremely upright in posture. . . . He had an easy rhythm in his conduct of large-scale selections: 'a nice-looking man with a stick [riding crop] in his hand . . . [who] . . . looked at the bodies and the faces [for] just a couple of seconds [and said] . . . left . . . right.'

[One line went straight to the gas chambers. The other went to the barracks, where they would be used as slave labor:] 'Some [witnesses] described a quality of playfulness . . . his "walking back and forth . . . [with a] cheerful expression on his face. . . . He was very playful. . . .'

[This playful manner could quickly give way to] 'outbreaks of rage and violence. . . . [In one case] . . . in which a mother did not want to be separated from her thirteen- or fourteen-year-old daughter, and bit and scratched the face of the SS man who tried to force her to her assigned line, Mengele drew his gun and shot both the woman and the child'."

than man, a creature so completely evil he could scarcely be considered human at all. His record shocked even Simon Wiesenthal, and that was not an easy thing to do.

Mengele was obsessed with the notion of breeding a race of "ideal Aryans." At the Auschwitz concentration camp, he studied the process of heredity by experimenting on identical twins. Whenever a transport arrived, Mengele checked the new arrivals for pairs of identical twins. When he found them, he took them into his personal custody. In his laboratory he was free to study them in any manner he chose.

As long as the twins were useful to him, Mengele saw to it that they received decent care. If his experiments demanded that he injure or even kill his subjects, he did not hesitate to do so.

He sometimes killed his subjects just to do autopsies—medical examinations after death—on them. A prisoner-doctor who was forced to assist Mengele told of one horrifying incident which he witnessed. Mengele assembled seven pairs of Gypsy twins in his work room. At about midnight, he had the first subject brought in to his dissecting room. He gave the girl an anesthetic to put her to sleep. Then, without a word to any of his assistants, he calmly injected chloroform directly into her heart. The girl died instantly—and Mengele called for the next victim. So it went throughout the night, until all fourteen children were dead.

A DESIRE FOR RETRIBUTION

Faced with this evil, Wiesenthal nearly broke his first rule of Nazi hunting: seek justice, not vengeance. It was difficult not to want revenge on such a man. Wiesenthal hunted him with anger and with passion.

Perhaps in this case, Wiesenthal's passion outstripped his judgment. He grabbed every scrap of information he could find. He released numerous reports of sightings that came to nothing. Time and again he claimed to be closing in on Mengele, only to lose him one more time.

These errors bothered many people. Mengele biographers Gerald L. Posner and John Ware wrote that Wiesenthal's "financial constraints and a knack of playing to the gallery . . . compromised his credibility."[62] Benno Varon, Israeli ambassador to Paraguay from 1968 to 1972, dismissed Wiesenthal's efforts in the Mengele investigation by saying that "Wiesenthal was always a Nazi hunter, but never a Nazi finder."[63]

In June 1985, the German government turned up evidence that Mengele drowned in 1979 in Brazil. Mengele's son Rolf confirmed the notice and told the authorities where his father was buried. An international team of experts examined the corpse and concluded that it was indeed Josef Mengele.

At first, Wiesenthal accepted the evidence. In his newsletter for January 11, 1986, he wrote that the case was concluded.[64] Later, he changed his mind, believing he had found errors in the examination. Not until 1992, when DNA testing confirmed the earlier findings, did Wiesenthal finally agree that the hunt for Mengele was over.

THE WOMAN CALLED KOBYLA

The women prisoners of the Majdanek death camp called Hermine Braunsteiner *Kobyla*, the mare, for her habit of kicking her victims. She was one of the most vicious guards at Majdanek, male or female.

Wiesenthal learned of her crimes during a visit to Tel Aviv in January 1964. Three women approached him in a sidewalk cafe and told about their experiences with Kobyla. One of the informants told of an incident that happened when a group of new arrivals were being processed into the camp:

> I'll never forget that child, the child. . . a small child, you know. . . . The man had it on his back. I mean, he had a rucksack on his back and one couldn't see what was inside. By sheer chance he came close to the Braunsteiner woman. She always had a whip with her when a new transport arrived. She lashed out with it wildly and hit the rucksack. At that moment we heard cries and sobs coming from it. She ordered the pack to be opened

at once, a child emerged. We were quite close and could see its face: it was very upset and tore itself loose from the man . . . and ran off. But Kobyla ran after it, grabbed it hard so it screamed, and fired a bullet through.[65]

The woman broke off, unable to continue. Kobyla had shot the child in the face.

On the strength of this testimony, Wiesenthal added the name of Hermine Braunsteiner to his ever-growing list. He discovered that she had served at the Ravensbrück concentration camp before her posting to Majdanek. A war crimes tribunal had tried and convicted her for crimes at Ravensbrück. She served three years in prison for those crimes without anyone connecting her to the equally terrible offenses at Majdanek.

Wiesenthal tracked Braunsteiner to Canada and finally to the United States.

CONFRONTING KOBYLA

On May 10, 1979, Holocaust survivor Hela Rosenbaum gave testimony at the war crimes trial of fifteen staff members of the Majdanek death camp. This transcript of Hela Rosenbaum's confrontation with Hermine Braunsteiner, the "Mare of Majdanek" is quoted in Kevin Mahoney's In Pursuit of Justice: Examining the Evidence of the Holocaust.

"Day 260. 10 May 1978. Following protocol [established courtroom procedure], the presiding judge asked the witness Hela Rosenbaum the question, 'Are any of the accused relatives of yours or related to you by marriage?' The woman, fifty-one years old, becomes bright red in the face. 'I am a Jew!' The judge explains to her why he must ask this question. The woman pulls nervously on her black velvet jacket. Finally, after she is again asked about any possible relation to the SS guards of Majdanek, she quietly answers, 'No, Thank God, no.'

Hela Rosenbaum can hardly control the tension that this reunion with the women SS guards has welled up inside her. As she stands in front of the accused Hermine Braunsteiner-Ryan, she is only able to choke out, 'Kobyla, that's Kobyla.' Then the presiding judge has to interrupt the proceedings. A doctor treats the overexcited woman. Twenty minutes later she is standing in front of Hildegard Lächert. 'Bloody Brygida. Never without her whip,' she says. Once she received twenty-five lashes from her. She describes that, then pauses. The judge asks her a question. She does not answer. He asks her again. Hela Rosenbaum says, 'Excuse me please, I am no longer here, Your Honor. I am back in the camp.'"

He found her in New York, married to an American construction worker and living the life of a respectable housewife and mother. From all appearances, there was no trace of the infamous Kobyla in Hermine Braunsteiner-Ryan. She had not only made a new life, she had become a different person. Her neighbors described her as kind and gentle; a woman who was not given to anger, let alone brutality.

Wiesenthal's attitude toward Braunsteiner-Ryan revealed a great deal about his notions of justice. Many people who learned of her crimes wondered what dark, inner realities had transformed Hermine Braunsteiner into Kobyla, the mare of Majdanek. Had she led a hard life? Was she ever mistreated by Jews? Did something inside her snap when she found herself in the brutal world of a concentration camp?

Wiesenthal could not answer those questions, nor did he think it important to try: "any criminal act has some ultimate explanation in the criminal's [mind]. But that doesn't make the action any better. We have to go by actions."[66]

Justice demanded that evil actions be punished. To Wiesenthal, it was just that simple. Whatever Braunsteiner-Ryan had been before the war, whatever she had become after it, did not matter. The actions at Majdanek spoke for themselves.

Getting her extradited from the United States and tried in Germany was a long, drawn-out process. Wiesenthal patiently

Infamously cruel Majdanek prison guard Hermine Braunsteiner-Ryan was sentenced to life imprisonment in June 1981.

worked through every stage of that process. On June 30, 1981, Hermine Braunsteiner-Ryan was sentenced to life imprisonment for her deeds at Majdanek.

Simon Wiesenthal put another case into his "completed" file. Then he turned his attention back to the war crimes list. There were still hundreds of criminals to pursue.

6 To the Ends of the Earth

During his long career, Simon Wiesenthal never failed to make an impact on those around him. People either idolized him or detested him. It was hard to find a middle ground where the world's most famous Nazi hunter was concerned. He had always been driven, rigid in his opinions, egotistical, and fiercely independent. These characteristics did not mellow as he grew older. They earned him many enemies, but they also made him good at his work.

THE ODESSA FILE

Wiesenthal was accustomed to having members of the press and the media come to his office. He was not accustomed to meeting bestselling novelists. He did not know what to think when Frederick Forsythe asked to see him.

Forsythe was an American who wrote spy novels and political thrillers. When he decided to write about ODESSA, he turned to Simon Wiesenthal for help. He had an idea for the hero of the book: a young Gentile who gets involved in Nazi hunting to learn the truth about his father's death. All he needed was a villain.

He wanted Wiesenthal to help him create a character that would be believable and authentic.

The veteran Nazi hunter had another idea. Why not use a real person? It should not be one of the famous war criminals. That would bind the story too tightly to the known facts of a particular person's life. Someone "relatively [unknown], but nasty,"[67] would be better. Wiesenthal suggested Eduard Roschmann, the butcher of Riga.

As second in command of the Riga ghetto, Roschmann was directly responsible for the murder of at least 3,800 people. He deported many more to the gas chambers at Auschwitz.

Forsythe agreed that Roschmann was a suitably evil subject. Wiesenthal gave him details about the ghetto and suggested the names of survivors who might be willing to share their experiences. The two men worked together for three days, creating an accurate background for Forsythe's fictional characters.

Twice more, they got together to compare notes and exchange ideas. Both men gained from these meetings. Forsythe got his villain and Wiesenthal got a means of smoking Roschmann out of hiding.

An anonymous tip to the Argentinean police led to Roschmann's arrest. He was later released on condition that he leave the country. Roschmann fled to Paraguay, where he soon died of a heart attack.

Though Roschmann was never tried for his crimes, Wiesenthal considered the case a success. The butcher of Riga had died knowing that the story of his crimes was playing in theaters all over the world. It was a peculiar form of justice, to be sure, but it was satisfying nonetheless.

A Case of "Mistaken Identity"

Wiesenthal's sense of justice did not include anything so crude as the end justi-

Frederick Forsythe, author of The Odessa File.

fying the means. But that did not stop him from using an occasional deception to gain his ends. In the case of Gustav Wagner, he decided that one small deception was justified.

Wagner was a big, brutal man. According to Wiesenthal, he looked "like a picture-book SS man, with huge shoulders and enormous hands."[68] He began his SS career at the Schloss Hartheim euthanasia center, where he worked with Franz Stangl. Later, both men were transferred to Sobibor. Stangl moved on to Treblinka, but Wagner remained at Sobibor, where he was promoted to deputy commandant.

As part of his duties, Wagner took personal charge of the gas chambers. It was his duty to see that they worked efficiently and were always filled to capacity. This he did with pleasure. He pounced on any prisoner who resisted, broke ranks, or simply collapsed on the way into the gas chamber. He liked to kill such troublemakers with his bare hands.

In 1978, Wiesenthal happened to see a photo of a party in Brazil. A group of old Nazis had gathered to celebrate the eighty-ninth anniversary of Adolf Hitler's birth. Wiesenthal scanned the photo for signs of a familiar face. He found none, but he began to wonder: might Gustav Wagner have been at that party? A number of sources had reported that Wagner lived in Brazil.

Maybe he appeared in other photographs. Wiesenthal decided to investigate. As usual, he lacked funds to make a trip, but a chance meeting in Israel

FREDERICK FORSYTHE ON SIMON WIESENTHAL

Wiesenthal biographer Hella Pick interviewed the Odessa File *author about his meetings with Wiesenthal. Pick quoted Forsythe's comments in her book* Simon Wiesenthal: A Life in Search of Justice.

"I turned to . . . Simon Wiesenthal [because] I wanted his advice on constructing my villain. . . . Wiesenthal didn't know who I was, and had not heard of *The Day of the Jackal* [Forsythe's previous bestselling novel]. He had no particular reason for giving me of his time. But he was delighted when he realised that I could speak German—his English then was still very halting—and he became very animated when I outlined my plot line.

'Why use a fictional character?' Wiesenthal asked. He had 200 names on his files who might fit my bill, and argued that a commandant from one of the concentration camps in Eastern Europe would be best. He discarded the best-known names and said it would be better to take someone relatively obscure, but nasty. He proposed Roschmann."

provided him with an opportunity. A Brazilian journalist agreed to check his newspaper's files for all available material.

Wiesenthal returned to Vienna, greatly encouraged by the meeting. The journalist not only found another photo of the party, but a complete guest list as well. He brought the material to Wiesenthal's office. Wiesenthal examined the list and looked at the photo with a magnifying glass. No Gustav Wagner.

Wiesenthal was sure, because an informant had given him copies of Wagner's Red Cross Passport and Brazilian identity card. He had held these documents for years, just waiting for the chance to match them with a lead.

Now that the chance had come, he did not intend to let it go. At that point, he

decided to take a gamble. He picked a man in the photo, almost at random, and identified him as Wagner: "I wasn't sure whether [this] was . . . quite legal. But the murder of 150,000 Jews at Sobibor and the attitude of the Brazilian authorities justified my actions in my own conscience."[69]

The identification made front page news in Brazil: Brazilians were outraged to learn that the former deputy commandant of Sobibor was living among them as a free man. Wiesenthal relates how they demanded action:

> [The story] was taken up by the radio and [spread] throughout the country. The police had no hope of remaining inactive, even though the man I had

described vigorously, and rightly, protested that it was all a mistake. Somehow [the police] had to find Gustav Wagner.[70]

A WANTED MAN

Wagner's passport and identity card photos appeared in newspapers all over the country: "[Wagner] saved the police their work. Evidently worn down by constant flight and weary of hiding . . . he surrendered to the authorities."[71]

Once Wagner was in custody, the extradition battle began. Germany wanted Wagner because he had been in the SS. Austria wanted him because he had been at Schoss Hartheim, Poland because he had worked at Sobibor, and Israel because most of his victims were Jews. In 1979, the Brazilian Supreme Court turned down all these requests for various technical reasons.

Wagner was released from custody, but like Eduard Roschmann he did not benefit from his freedom. He was hounded by the press. When detailed reports of his crimes hit the newspapers, even other Germans turned away from him. In October 1979, he fled to a remote farm where he hanged himself.

THE KREISKY "WARS"

One of Wiesenthal's firmest principles was that ex-Nazis should not be allowed to hold public office. In 1970, this position brought him into conflict with Bruno Kreisky, the newly elected chancellor of Austria. By political affiliation, Kreisky was a socialist; by birth, he was a Jew.

Kreisky was not a religious Jew, nor was he a Zionist (one who favors Jewish resettlement in Palestine, an activist for the state of Israel). He called himself "an Austrian of Jewish origin"[72] and made it clear that his first loyalty was to his Austrian homeland. He once told an Israeli journalist that "The Jews are not a [separate] people, and if they are, they are a lousy people."[73]

Such statements were guaranteed to offend Simon Wiesenthal. Being a Jewish Holocaust survivor was the central fact of his life. That someone like Kreisky could

The chancellor of Austria, Bruno Kreisky, attempted to appoint four ex-Nazis to his cabinet of advisers.

turn away from his heritage was an insult to the six million and to Jews everywhere.

Perhaps because he knew that his opinions would carry no weight with Bruno Kreisky, Wiesenthal kept his feelings to himself. He might never have spoken out if Kreisky had not appointed four former Nazis to his first cabinet. One of these men, Minister of Agriculture Hans Öllinger, was not just a Nazi but a former lieutenant in the SS.

When Wiesenthal revealed this information to the press, the world was outraged. Kreisky was furious. Rather than admit that he had made a mistake with Öllinger, Kreisky defended him. This led to further investigations and more recriminations. Kreisky and Wiesenthal fought a war of words, with the press in the middle.

Kreisky went on record that Nazis, including former SS men, could serve in public office so long as they had no criminal records. To support this position, he used one of Wiesenthal's favorite themes: collective guilt does not serve the ends of justice.

Wiesenthal's response was short and to the point: "I am against the theory of collective guilt, but I am also against the theory of collective innocence. Not even the Jews have collective innocence."[74]

"Wiesenthal's law" applied to former Nazis in the same way it applied to Jews who served in ghetto governments: neither should have positions of authority in the postwar world. On this point, Wiesenthal was firm, and he would not be silent.

THE PETER SCANDAL

Before the Austrian elections of October 1975, the feud between Wiesenthal and Kreisky found a new focus. It started when Wiesenthal spotted a familiar name on a roster of the First SS Infantry Brigade.

The First SS was an execution squad that followed the regular army into the Soviet Union. In 1941–1942, the First SS massacred 13,497 "Jews, gypsies, partisans, bandits, and suspected enemies."[75]

The name Wiesenthal found was that of Friedrich Peter—the man who was likely to become vice chancellor in Bruno Kreisky's next government.

In Austria's parliamentary system there are many political parties. It often happens that no single party will win a majority of the vote. In order to build a governing majority, the largest party must make coalitions, or alliances, with others. This involves tradeoffs. The tradeoff Kreisky proposed was to make Peter the vice chancellor in return for the support of Friedrich Peter's Freedom Party.

Wiesenthal found this intolerable. He took his information to Austrian president Dr. Rudolf Kirchschläger. The two men agreed not to go public until after the elections, which were a week away. To do otherwise might cause a backlash. If voters decided that the attack on Peter was politically motivated, they might vote for him in protest.

Although the Austrian presidency was and is largely a ceremonial office, Kirchschläger did have one important power: he could accept or reject any government. If he refused to seat a particular set of officials, he could call for new elections.

Kirchschläger assured Wiesenthal that he would not allow Friedrich Peter to become vice chancellor. He informed both Kreisky and Peter of that decision and sent them each a copy of Wiesenthal's evidence.

As it happened, Kreisky's party won a clear majority in the October elections; there was no need for coalitions. The danger was over, but neither Wiesenthal nor Kirchschläger believed it was over for good. At some time in the future, Kreisky might still work with Peter.

THE BATTLE HEATS UP

To prevent any future coalitions between Kreisky and Peter, Wiesenthal decided to go public with his findings. On October 9, 1975, he held a press conference to reveal Peter's war record. Kreisky's reaction was swift and terrible. He questioned Wiesenthal's methods, his morality, and his right to Austrian citizenship. He even hinted that Wiesenthal had survived the Holocaust by cooperating in some way with the Nazis.

Wiesenthal was outraged. That such charges should be leveled at him was more than he could bear. To add to the indignity, the Austrian people overwhelmingly backed Kreisky. Wiesenthal stood alone.

Lawsuits for defamation of character flew back and forth in the courts. Peter sued Wiesenthal for slander. For good measure, he also sued two magazines that printed unfavorable articles about his war record.

Wiesenthal tried to bring an action against Kreisky, but Austrian law does not allow a private citizen to sue a public official. For his part, Kreisky mounted an investiga-tion on Wiesenthal's wartime activities. The situation between the two men grew worse over the years.

In April 1986, Kreisky gave an interview to the Austrian magazine *Profil*. When the reporter asked about his attacks on Wiesenthal in 1975, Kreisky bristled. Everything he had said was true, he insisted. He could have proved Wiesenthal's wartime misconduct, "but I simply was not in the mood at that time to stand before a judge and depend on former Nazis as my witnesses."[76] Once more, Kreisky offered neither evidence nor detail to support his charges.

Wiesenthal sued again. This time the case went to court because Kreisky was retired and no longer shielded by parliamentary immunity. In a dramatic trial that dragged on until October 1989, the court found Kreisky guilty of slander. The judge fined the former chancellor 270,000 shillings (about $20,000) and asked him to make a formal apology for his actions. This Kreisky refused to do. He died on July 29, 1990, without having made his peace with Simon Wiesenthal.

THE LOS ANGELES CONNECTION

Although Wiesenthal's battle with Kreisky cost him support in Austria, it did not have a similar effect in other countries. He was invited to speak at important functions, given honorary degrees by prestigious institutions, and generally admired for his unswerving dedication to his work.

In 1977, Rabbi Marvin Hier of Los Angeles telephoned Wiesenthal with an

Wiesenthal in his Vienna office in 1992, still on the hunt for hidden Nazis.

idea. He wanted to establish a Holocaust study center in Los Angeles. Rather than go into details over the phone, he asked to meet with Wiesenthal.

At that meeting, the Simon Wiesenthal Center for Holocaust Studies was born. Though it would carry Wiesenthal's name, he would not be directly involved with its operation. He would, however, be kept informed of its activities.

In 1978, Wiesenthal went to Los Angeles to help launch the center. At that time the center was only an idea that existed on paper and in the minds of a few visionaries. Fortunately for the organizers, the idea proved to be a timely one. In rapid succession, three events raised public interest in the Holocaust: a neo-Nazi group won the right to parade through the streets of Skokie, Illinois; the mini-series *Holocaust* appeared on American television; and Germany considered placing a statute of limitations on Nazi war crimes.

These events raised questions that people could not answer. "Suddenly, the media, teachers, clergy and parents turned to the Center for guidance and perspective. As a result, the Outreach program was launched—a full year before the Center's Holocaust museum would open."[77]

WIESENTHAL AND THE SKOKIE NAZIS

Simon Wiesenthal's reaction to the Skokie parade showed a side of him that surprised some people. The parade was scheduled for April 20, 1978—Adolf Hitler's birthday. Twenty young Nazis planned to march through the streets of Skokie, dressed in Nazi uniforms and carrying swastika flags. Such a parade would have been a shock in any American town. In Skokie, it was an outrage. A large number of Holocaust survivors had settled there. For them, the parade was a nightmare from the past come back to life.

Protests over the parade had no effect. The American Civil Liberties Union (ACLU) defended the Nazis' right to march, based upon the First Amendment to the Constitution, which guaranteed freedom of speech and assembly.

The members of Chicago's Jewish Federation decided to stage a massive counterdemonstration. The Nazis would have twenty men marching through Skokie. They would have five thousand Jews marching through Chicago.

Wiesenthal happened to be speaking in Chicago at that time, so he was included in the discussions. He did not agree that a huge march would be the best response. Ignore the Nazi parade, he said, or better yet, make fun of it. Ridicule could be a

THE BIRTH OF THE SIMON WIESENTHAL CENTER

In Response, *the magazine of the Simon Wiesenthal Center, Rabbi Marvin Hier described his feelings as he prepared to open the new facility.*

"I can still remember the day . . . we first took possession of the building at 9760 W. Pico Blvd. It was so large and bare and had been stripped of its light fixtures. In order to communicate with the world, we installed a single telephone with a long extension cord which I took with me whenever I moved through the building. . . . It's still hard to imagine that from those origins grew the Simon Wiesenthal Center and the Museum of Tolerance.

But none of these dreams could have become a reality without the consistent support and loyalty of so many dedicated people. It is a tribute to them that this important human rights institution is now very much a part of the fabric of American society.

The important thing to remember is that [our] liberties. . . are never free. . . . Speaking out against injustice and hatred is the rent all of us must pay in order to live in a better world. As Simon Wiesenthal said, 'Freedom is not a gift from heaven. . . . One must fight for it each and every day.'"

The Simon Wiesenthal Center for Holocaust Studies opened its doors in April 1979. In addition to an appearance by Wiesenthal himself, the opening ceremony featured speeches by Los Angeles mayor Tom Bradley, California governor Jerry Brown, and other notables.

WALDHEIM IN THE EYE OF THE STORM

In defending Austrian president Kurt Waldheim, Simon Wiesenthal stood almost entirely alone. Even when he called for Waldheim's resignation, he would not admit that the man was a war criminal. Attorney Eli M. Rosenbaum makes this clear in his book Betrayal: The Untold Story of the Kurt Waldheim Investigation and Cover-Up.

"[Wiesenthal] . . . denied that the evidence proved Waldheim's direct involvement in war crimes. But the Nazi-hunter made an unexpected and dramatic move [in October 1987]. For the first time, he called on Waldheim to resign the Austrian presidency. If the commission found Waldheim 'guilty,' Wiesenthal said, he would have to resign. And even if the commission cleared Waldheim, Wiesenthal said, he would still be 'a burden for Austria,' and should step down anyway. . . . A short time later, OSI's Neal Sher, along with U.S. Ambassador to Austria Ronald Lauder, encountered Wiesenthal at a . . . dinner in New York. The two American officials saw their chance to urge him to expand on his new position that Waldheim should resign. They proposed a statement for Wiesenthal to issue, denouncing Waldheim. A participant in the conversation called me . . . two days after the dinner. 'Simon wouldn't budge,' he reported. 'He won't do anything that might make it look like the WJC [which opposed Waldheim and criticized Wiesenthal] was right.'"

formidable weapon. Wiesenthal suggested that only twenty Jews should march in Chicago—but they should do it with a herd of pigs, wearing swastika bands around their bellies.

Though the federation members doubtless got a good laugh out of Wiesenthal's idea, they eventually chose to stage the mass march. On April 20, five thousand Jews marched in Chicago and sixteen Nazis (four of the original group decided not to attend) trudged through the streets of Skokie. The media had a field day. When it was over, neither the Jews nor the Nazis could say exactly what had been accomplished.

Life went back to normal. The *Holocaust* mini-series aired on television; the German government decided not to place a statute of limitation on war crimes; and Simon Wiesenthal returned to his work in Vienna.

THE WALDHEIM AFFAIR

In 1986, the World Jewish Congress (WJC) uncovered evidence that Austrian presidential candidate Kurt Waldheim had lied about his wartime career. That discovery triggered an investigation that would stun the world.

Waldheim was not just a national figure. As a former Secretary General of the United Nations (UN), he was known and respected all over the world. It was no secret that he had served in the German army during the war. According to his own statements, he was wounded in 1941 and placed on extended leave until the war was nearly over.

During his term as UN secretary general, there had been questions about Waldheim's wartime activities. In 1981, the Israeli representative to the UN silenced the rumors by stating publicly that his government gave Waldheim a clean bill of health. For most people, this was enough to settle the matter. If Waldheim had been involved in war crimes, surely the Israelis would be the first to condemn him.

Some time later, an amateur historian discovered an extraordinary photo. It showed then-lieutenant Waldheim with an SS general and two other high-ranking Nazi officers. The photo was taken on May 22, 1943, in Podgorica, Yugoslavia. That placed Waldheim on active duty during the time he had claimed to be home on extended leave. It also linked him to the notorious "Black Operation," a campaign in which thousands of Yugoslav partisans and other civilians lost their lives.

A 1947 report from the Yugoslavian War Crimes Commission

> contained page after page of frightful detail about the Black Operation: Prisoners were routinely executed by gunfire or, when the captors were Croats, often burned alive or hacked to pieces with knives and hatchets; innocent hostages were shot and hanged by the thousands; villages were destroyed, often with their entire populations trapped inside.[78]

Austrian president Kurt Waldheim was discovered to be an ex-Nazi and participator in the Black Operation.

WALDHEIM BECOMES PRESIDENT

The WJC began an investigation that made headlines all over the world. As the world's most famous authority on Nazi war criminals, Wiesenthal soon found himself in the middle of the debate. He defended Waldheim, saying that his military record showed no involvement in

Elie Wiesel, concentration camp survivor and winner of the 1986 Nobel Peace Prize.

war crimes. True, the Podgorica photo proved that Waldheim had tried to cover up his wartime activities. That might make the man a liar, but it did not make him a criminal.

Though the scandal broke just before the Austrian elections, it did not damage Waldheim's candidacy. He won the presidency by an overwhelming majority.

Wiesenthal continued to defend the new president, though governments and Jewish organizations all over the world were condemning him. Even the Simon Wiesenthal Center in Los Angeles got involved. Over Wiesenthal's objections, the center launched a campaign to have Waldheim barred from entering the United States.

They distributed thousands of postcards for people to mail. The cards showed the famous Podgorica picture beneath a headline: "America Says No to Waldheim."[79] On the back a preprinted message called upon President Ronald Reagan to place Kurt Waldheim on the watchlist of accused Nazi war criminals.

A COSTLY STAND

Wiesenthal realized that public furor over Waldheim had reached a point of no return. Nobody who was mired in such controversy could serve effectively in public life. Wiesenthal called upon the embattled president to resign for the good of Austria, but he still refused to believe that Waldheim was a war criminal. In the face of overwhelming evidence and world opinion, he stood firm. His stance would cost him dearly.

It placed him at odds with Jewish organizations all over the world. His link with the Los Angeles center that bore his name was nearly broken. Only an emotional conference with Rabbi Hier kept it intact. The always difficult relationship between his Vienna Documentation Center and the WJC was damaged beyond repair. Wiesenthal claimed that the WJC had made mistakes it was not prepared to admit. The WJC claimed that it was Wiesenthal who made the mistakes: his investigation of Waldheim had been incompetent.

Wiesenthal's role in the Waldheim case may even have cost him a Nobel Peace Prize. In 1986, both Wiesenthal and fellow survivor Elie Wiesel were nominated. Some people expected them to be named joint recipients. Instead, Wiesel alone received the award. Wiesenthal, who has never hidden his fondness for honors and awards, was deeply disappointed.

According to author and Wiesenthal critic Eli Rosenbaum, Wiesenthal blamed the WJC for his failure to share in the award: "[Wiesenthal] said he had heard that a letter to the Prize Committee from the WJC had effectively killed his candidacy."[80] The WJC denied writing any such letter.

In 1987, the United States government placed Waldheim on the watchlist. Other governments followed suit. The president of Austria was soon banned from dozens of countries around the world. Austria's image in the international community suffered as a result.

Pressured from all sides, Kurt Waldheim stepped down from the presidency at the end of his term in 1992. He still said he had done nothing wrong, and still noted that no less an authority than Simon Wiesenthal had supported him.

Chapter
7 In the Eye of the Storm

Wiesenthal's interests expanded in the 1980s. In addition to Nazi hunting, he became involved in human rights issues. He took an interest in all victims of genocide, and in people who were oppressed because they had dared to behave morally in the midst of immoral societies. One of his first such causes was that of Raoul Wallenberg, the Swedish diplomat who saved thousands of Hungarian Jews from the gas chambers.

THE HEROISM OF
RAOUL WALLENBERG

Simon Wiesenthal's involvement in the search for Raoul Wallenberg began in April 1971, with a letter from Wallenberg's mother. Wallenberg had disappeared into a Soviet prison after the war, but she believed he was still alive. Would Wiesenthal help to find him?

Wiesenthal knew the story. Raoul Wallenberg was a junior member of the Swedish legation, or diplomatic staff, when the Nazis took Budapest in October 1944. He knew what would happen to the city's Jews.

The Nazis recruited street toughs from the Hungarian fascist group Arrow Cross. Armed with German guns, these young men raged through Jewish neighborhoods. They attacked people in the streets and dragged them from their homes. They stormed into Swedish and Swiss "safe houses" and slaughtered all the occupants. Within twenty-four hours they had killed six hundred Jews.

The next day, they rounded up six thousand Jews and locked them into two synagogues. Other Jews were trapped inside their homes, unable to buy food or get medical attention. In the face of this need, Wallenberg went into action. He bought food and medicine with money supplied by a Jewish welfare agency and recruited young people to deliver the supplies. He also found forty doctors who inoculated the imprisoned Jews against diseases such as typhoid fever and cholera.

When the Nazis began deporting Jews to the death camps, Wallenberg handed out thousands of Swedish passports. He then used his diplomatic status to insist that these Swedish "citizens" be granted protected status. He saved as many as one hundred thousand people in this way.

When the Soviet army closed on Budapest, the Nazis fled. Wallenberg and those who helped him should have been safe in "liberated" Budapest. They were not. On January 17, 1945, the Soviets arrested Wallenberg on undetermined charges. Some sources believe he was accused of black-market activities. Others claim the charge was espionage (spying), either for the Germans or for the Americans.

Swedish diplomat Raoul Wallenberg used his social status to hand out Swedish citizenship papers to thousands of Jews.

THE MYSTERY OF RAOUL WALLENBERG

Whatever the charge, Wallenberg disappeared. The man who had saved thousands slipped through the cracks of history and was lost. Rumors of his whereabouts continued to surface for many years. Reliable witnesses claimed he was being held in a Soviet prison, but inquiries from the U.S. and Swedish governments produced no results. In time, Raoul Wallenberg was all but forgotten.

Then Simon Wiesenthal came along. By tracing Wallenberg's movements through the Soviet prison system, he became convinced that Wallenberg was indeed alive. When his efforts to make contact led only to dead ends, Wiesenthal resorted to his old standby: publicity. He set out to create a public clamor over the case.

His approach was not systematic. Although Wiesenthal had a knack for drawing attention to his cases, he was not a professional publicist. He began in the simplest way possible, by scheduling a press conference. He told a roomful of reporters what he knew and why he believed that the Soviets were holding Wallenberg. The resulting headlines aroused interest in the story.

When even the Swedish government gave up hope that Wallenberg could be found alive, Wiesenthal refused to quit. Wallenberg's mother died in 1979, never having learned what happened to her son. Still, Wiesenthal continued the probe. As late as 1991, he was saying that "Raoul Wallenberg is alive so long as the Russians don't give us believable information about his death."[81]

During the Wallenberg investigation, Wiesenthal got a firsthand look at the human rights abuses of the Soviet Union. He did not like what he saw. In 1975, he became involved with an international group that was formed to investigate Soviet human rights violations in general and the plight of dissident physicist Andrei Sakharov in particular.

THE ORDEAL OF ANDREI SAKHAROV

In the early 1950s, Andrei Sakharov led the team of Soviet scientists who developed the hydrogen bomb. By the late 1950s, he began to realize that he had created a monster. The arms race between the United States and the Soviet Union had gotten out of hand. People lived under the dark threat of thermonuclear war. Radioactive fallout from atomic testing

REMEMBERING RAOUL WALLENBERG

Swedish author Jan Larsson described the courage and daring of Raoul Wallenberg in "Swedish Portraits," a chapter in his book on Sweden.

"By now, people in most parts of the world have heard about Raoul Wallenberg's extraordinary rescue action on behalf of the Hungarian Jews during World War II. . . . During my lecture tours both in Sweden and abroad . . . I have often been asked how it was possible to save such a large number of people—about 100,000—from the Nazi executioners. The most important answer: Raoul Wallenberg was the right man in the right place, given the situation then prevailing. Although he was not the heroic type in the ordinary sense, he was a fearless, skilled negotiator and organizer. He was, moreover, a good actor, a talent that served him well during his clashes with the Nazis. He could also show two different personalities. The first was the calm, humorous, intellectual, warm person that we co-workers could see. The second was Raoul Wallenberg in confrontation with the Nazis: he was transformed into an aggressive person who would shout at them or threaten them on one occasion, flatter or bribe them on another. . . . They were impressed by him and usually gave in to his demands. One reason, of course, was his Swedish diplomatic status, which the Germans did not dare to violate."

Soviet scientist Andrei Sakharov was held under house arrest for his emotional appeals to end the arms race.

had become a worldwide health threat. Sakharov took a stand: the arms race should stop, he said. He became an outspoken advocate for disarmament and limits on nuclear testing.

This courageous stand earned him a Nobel Peace Prize in 1975. He was honored almost everywhere except in his homeland. There he was regarded as dangerous. Instead of becoming more cautious in his statements, he began speaking out on human rights issues as well as nuclear disarmament. His activities soon attracted unwelcome attention from the Soviet Secret Police (KGB).

In 1980, Sakharov was placed under house arrest. For six long years, he and his wife Elena Bonner were prisoners in their own apartment. A twenty-four-hour KGB guard stood watch outside their door. Their every move was monitored. They had no telephone, no visitors, little contact with the outside world. Occasionally they were allowed to leave the apartment for brief periods, but a KGB escort always went along. This house arrest, or "internal exile," prevented Sakharov from speaking out, but it could not change his opinions. He remained a staunch foe of Soviet nuclear policy and Soviet repression.

Both Sakharov and his wife suffered from heart conditions. Sakharov made his condition worse by several hunger strikes, protests against government injustice and inaction. According to writer Patricia Blake, Soviet authorities responded to these strikes with "forced feedings and deliberately inadequate medical care." One doctor was quite frank about the intent of these treatments: "We won't let you die, but we will make you an invalid,"[82] he told Sakharov.

WIESENTHAL AND SAKHAROV

Simon Wiesenthal was impressed by Sakharov's courage. Probably he saw in this Russian dissident a reflection of himself. Both men championed unpopular causes. Both defied their own governments, and both paid the price of that defiance.

Wiesenthal not only saw parallels between himself and Sakharov, but between the Nazis and the Soviets. In 1975, he was invited to join a committee of the newly formed International Sakharov Hearings. The hearings had a two-fold purpose: to win freedom for Sakharov and to investigate human rights violations in the Soviet Union.

At the first hearing in October 1975, the topic was Soviet gulags (prison camps). The picture that emerged was painfully familiar to Wiesenthal: starvation, slave labor, brutal guards:

> To anyone who has ever been in a concentration camp, any camp anywhere on earth is a festering wound: if I think of a person lying on his bunk in a Soviet camp then he is at that moment my fellow inmate, and anything inflicted on him is being inflicted on me.[83]

Andrei Sakharov was finally released in 1986, after Mikhail Gorbachev came to power in the Soviet Union. Two years later, he and Simon Wiesenthal met for the first time. These two champions of human rights did not come together at some grand public occasion, but in the home of a mutual friend. There were no rallies, no banners, no stirring speeches, just dinner and quiet conversation. "It was a most happy moment for me,"[84] said Wiesenthal.

Andrei Sakharov died the next year, on December 14, 1989. He had attended a meeting of a political action group that day. He returned home exhausted, but still fired with enthusiasm. The next day's agenda included debate on a nationwide strike against communist domination of the country. "Tomorrow there will be battle!"[85] Sakharov told his wife.

He never got to see that battle. He died before morning of a massive heart attack. He was sixty-eight years old.

Andrei Sakharov lived long enough to see the beginning of changes in his homeland. He had the satisfaction of knowing that he had been part of those changes, that his contribution to human rights would be remembered.

Simon Wiesenthal understood the importance of remembrance. The knowledge that one's sufferings would not be forgotten somehow made them easier to bear. He had worked a lifetime to give that feeling to other victims of oppression.

For Wiesenthal, "other victims" was a broad category. It included, for example, the millions of non-Jews who perished in the Holocaust. He was especially interested in the Gypsies.

THE GYPSY HOLOCAUST

Gypsies have their own name for the Holocaust. They call it "the devouring."[86] Their fate under the Nazis was similar to that of the Jews. Both were targeted for extermination on racial grounds.

Long before the Nazis came to power, Gypsies were hated and feared throughout Europe. They were the ultimate outsiders, rejecting everything that conventional society held dear. Gypsies lived as they pleased, traveling from place to place in their colorful caravans. They had no settled homes, no regular jobs, no respect for outside authority. For generations, they had roamed over Europe and nobody had been able to control them.

In the Nazi state, a people that could not be controlled could only be eliminated. SS leader Heinrich Himmler made this position clear in a statement on the Nazi attitude toward Gypsies: "Experiences gained in the struggle against the Gypsy plague and knowledge derived from race-biological research have shown that . . . the final solution of the Gypsy question . . . must be approached with the basic nature of this race in mind."[87] That statement was a death warrant for half a million Gypsies; more than two-thirds of the Gypsy population of Europe.

Simon Wiesenthal learned of the Gypsy tragedy in 1964, while he was examining a newly discovered archive of Nazi materials. He knew he had made an important discovery when he saw a familiar name: Adolf Eichmann. Eichmann himself had organized the transports that took thousands of Gypsies to the death camps.

For years, Wiesenthal followed the evidence trail. In the dry language of transport orders, requisition forms, and camp status reports it led him to a single conclusion: the Gypsies had been victims of genocide.

To Wiesenthal's dismay, nobody seemed to care. German authorities re-fused to act. Jewish leaders showed little sympathy for the Gypsies who had shared their fate. They were used to thinking of the Holocaust as a uniquely Jewish tragedy. For some survivors and Holocaust historians, acknowledging non-Jewish victims diminished that uniqueness.

It is possible that some of the resistance to Wiesenthal's message had more to do with the man himself than with the Gypsies. Wiesenthal's fierce independence, along with an almost arrogant confidence

Besides the Jews, thousands of Poles, Slavs, and Gypsies also lost their lives to the Nazis.

PORTRAIT OF A GYPSY

In her book Bury Me Standing, *author Isabel Fonseca captured the flavor of Gypsy life in her description of singer-poet Bronislawa Wajs.*

"Her real name was Bronislawa Wajs, but she is known by her Gypsy name, Papusza: 'Doll.' Papusza was one of the greatest Gypsy singers and poets ever and, for a while, one of the most celebrated. She lived all her life in Poland, and when she died in 1987 nobody noticed.

Like most Polish Gypsies, Papusza's family was nomadic—part of a great *kumpania,* or band of families, traveling with horses and in caravans, with the men at the front and the women and children following behind in open carts. Some of the richer families had elaborately carved hard-top caravans with narrow glass windows, sometimes diamond-shaped and set in painted wood frames. There might be as many as twenty caravans in the *kumpania.* Men, women, children, horses, carts, dogs: until the mid-1960s they moved along, down from Vilnius, through the eastern forests of Volhynia . . . crossing into the Tatra mountains in the south."

in his own findings, had earned him many enemies. As Wiesenthal's biographer pointed out, "Jewish leaders . . . were already critical of [him] as a lone ranger who was forever inserting himself into controversial Jewish affairs."[88]

The criticism stung Wiesenthal, but it did not stop him. His sense of justice demanded that non-Jewish victims be recognized and their killers punished. He pursued this goal with his usual passion. When officials would not listen, he went to the press. He gave interviews about the fate of the Gypsies, wrote articles, and publicized the Gypsy genocide in his Documentation Center newsletter.

In 1985, the German Jewish community planned a ceremony to mark the fortieth anniversary of the liberation of Bergen-Belsen. No Gypsies were included on the program, but Wiesenthal saw to it that they would not be entirely ignored. He convinced Chancellor Helmut Kohl, who was speaking at the ceremonies, to pay tribute to the Gypsy victims.

WIESENTHAL VS. WIESEL

Wiesenthal's activities on behalf of the Gypsies led to conflict with Elie Wiesel. On the surface, the two men appeared to have much in common. Both were Holocaust survivors. Both came from Eastern European backgrounds. Both lost their families in the camps. And both were determined that the world should not forget the horror they had experienced. There the similarities ended.

Wiesenthal tends to be confrontational. He is not always tactful in his dealings with other people. Wiesel is more restrained and therefore less likely to make enemies. Wiesenthal focuses on justice; Wiesel, on memory. This difference shows in their writings. For example, Wiesel's 1960 book, *Night,* is a powerful and deeply personal account of his experiences at Auschwitz. Wiesenthal's 1967 *The Murderers Among Us* focuses more on Nazi hunting than his own time in the camps.

In 1985, the two men were rivals for the Nobel Prize and opponents in the Kurt Waldheim controversy. They soon found themselves at odds over the Gypsies as well. Wiesel was president of the United States Holocaust Memorial Council, the group responsible for the Holocaust Memorial Museum in Washington, D.C. It included Polish, Russian, and Ukrainian members, but not a single Gypsy.

Wiesenthal wrote two letters to Wiesel. The first requested that a Gypsy be appointed to the council. The second all but demanded it. When Wiesel did not respond, Wiesenthal turned to the supporters of his Documentation Center.

He called upon them to flood Wiesel's office with mail. Wiesel did not take kindly to this pressure. The two men were already at odds over Kurt Waldheim, and both were keenly aware of their rivalry for the Nobel Peace Prize. Wiesenthal's tactics in the Gypsy matter widened the gulf between them.

Elie Wiesel did eventually acknowledge the Gypsy victims, but he never reconciled with the man who had championed their cause. Wiesenthal, for his part, spoke bitterly about Wiesel, when he bothered to speak at all.

WIESENTHAL UNDER FIRE

Along with the loss of the Nobel Prize, Wiesenthal faced other disappointments in the 1980s and 1990s. Partly as a legacy of the Waldheim case, his record as a champion of justice came under fire.

Wiesenthal had long been accused of inflating his role in many cases. For example, in his 1967 book *The Murderers Among Us,* Wiesenthal says that sending Max Diamant to find a photo of Adolf Eichmann was his idea. Diamant himself later told Wiesenthal's biographer that Simon "had nothing to do with the discovery of the photograph."[89] In 1973, German war crimes prosecutor Joachim Richter claimed that Wiesenthal's reports on Martin Bormann "contained [mostly] anonymous and frivolous-sounding letters."[90] In 1975, Isser Harel, leader of the team that arrested Adolf Eichmann, denied that Wiesenthal's information had any role in the operation.

Wiesenthal called Harel's words "an assault on the credibility of my Documentation Centre . . . the capture of Eichmann was a mosaic, a picture puzzle, and in it I had my place. Harel is trying to deny me this and I protest this."[91]

ELIE WIESEL REMEMBERS

In a book simply entitled Night, *Elie Wiesel recalled his arrival at the Auschwitz concentration camp.*

"Through the window [of the train car] we could see barbed wire; we realized that this must be the camp. . . . Suddenly we heard terrible screams:

'Jews, look! Look through the window! Flames! Look!'

And as the train stopped, we saw . . . that flames were gushing out of a tall chimney into the black sky. . . . We looked at the flames in the darkness. There was an abominable odor floating in the air. Suddenly, our doors opened. Some odd-looking characters, dressed in striped shirts and black trousers leapt into the wagon. . . . They began to strike out to right and left, shouting: 'Everybody get out! . . . Quickly!'

We jumped out. . . . In front of us flames. In the air that smell of burning flesh. It must have been about midnight. We had arrived—at Birkenau, reception center for Auschwitz."

In 1993, Eli Rosenbaum wrote a stinging criticism of Wiesenthal in his book on the Waldheim scandal. He not only called Wiesenthal's stand on Waldheim into question, but claimed that "Wiesenthal's roles in the biggest Nazi cases of all— Mengele, Bormann, and in all likelihood, Eichmann as well—were studies in ineptitude, exaggeration, and self-glorification."[92]

These attacks hurt Wiesenthal more deeply than he cared to admit. He reacted with anger and bitterness, often railing at the unfairness of his enemies. His daughter Paulinka recalled his "sleepless nights" and "deep anguish" over conflicts with other Jews.[93]

Paulinka Wiesenthal married at the age of nineteen and eventually went to live in Israel. Though she loves and respects her father, she is not blind to his faults. She knows he can be rigid and uncompromising. She also knows "that he has a big ego and . . . treasures the honours he has been awarded."[94] He enjoys meeting famous people. This does not diminish him in her eyes. It only makes him human.

AGAIN THE SUNFLOWER

Moving from crisis to crisis took its toll on Simon Wiesenthal. After being overlooked for the Nobel Peace Prize in 1986, he reexamined his life and work. Had he done enough? Had he been faithful to his mission? Wiesenthal explored these questions in his second autobiography, *Justice Not Vengeance*. Written in his eightieth year, this book covered much of the same material as the earlier *The Murderers Among Us.* The tone was different, however.

Wiesenthal at eighty was more reflective than he had been in 1967, at the age of fifty-eight. *The Murderers Among Us* was the work of a man in mid career. *Justice Not Vengeance* looked back on a lifetime. It summed up Wiesenthal's work, answered his critics, and explained his side of many controversies.

On the first page of the Preface, Wiesenthal indirectly dealt with one of the most persistent and troubling claims: that he was a glory hound who took credit for other people's work:

> [One] problem about a book like this is that it creates the impression that I

alone am responsible for all the successes and failures of the cases reported here. This is partly due to its presentation in the first person singular, and partly to the peculiarity of my work: security considerations compel me to sketch my colleagues as vaguely as possible. If I receive a strictly confidential piece of information from Paraguay it will be obvious to everybody that this is not the result of clairvoyance on my part, but that someone is working for me there, someone whom I would jeopardize by naming, or even by relating how he came by this information.[95]

Eight years after publication of *Justice Not Vengeance*, Wiesenthal returned to yet another theme from his past, forgiveness. In 1997, he published an expanded version of his 1970 book *The Sunflower*. Once more, he confronted the issues he had raised in

Auschwitz survivor Elie Wiesel, president of the United States Holocaust Memorial Center.

Wiesenthal sits in his office, content with the knowledge that he has brought dozens of murderers to justice and has never forgotten the 6 million Jews who lost their lives.

that long-ago encounter with a dying Nazi soldier. Even in his eighty-eighth year, the questions still nagged. Had he done the right thing? What in fact were the limits of forgiveness? What was the connection between forgiveness and justice?

Wiesenthal is neither philosopher, scholar, nor moralist. He would rather live his answers than try to put them into words. Passion matters more to him than professionalism; he has never been, nor claimed to be, a coolly detached investigator. He is a deeply emotional man with a fine sense of the dramatic, who perhaps tends to state his opinions as facts and his ideas as accomplishments. This has led to many misunderstandings along the way.

Detractors may question his record, but even they cannot deny his impact. Simon Wiesenthal has become a living legend. At a time when people wanted to forget the Holocaust, he made them remember. His work honored the victims, gave survivors the hope of justice, and caused many a Nazi fugitive to live in constant fear of discovery. When all is said and done, that is an enviable record.

Notes

Introduction: Speaker for the Dead

1. Quoted in A. James Rudin, "Since 1945, Nazi Hunter Wiesenthal Has Never Forgotten He's a 'Survivor,'" *Sacramento Bee*, January 16, 1999, *Scene* p. 5.

2. Simon Wiesenthal, *Justice Not Vengeance*. New York: Grove Weidenfeld, 1989, p. 1.

3. Quoted in Jordan Bofante, "War Crimes: Where Have All the Nazis Gone?" *Time*, August 9, 1993, p. 38.

Chapter 1: Ordinary Dreams

4. Alan Levy, *The Wiesenthal File*. Grand Rapids, MI: William B. Eerdmans Publishing, 1993, p. 24.

5. Quoted in Levy, *The Wiesenthal File*, p. 24.

6. Peter Michael Lingens, "Who Is Simon Wiesenthal?" in Wiesenthal, *Justice Not Vengeance*, p. 3.

7. Lingens, "Who Is Simon Wiesenthal?" p. 3.

8. Quoted in Hella Pick, *Simon Wiesenthal: A Life in Search of Justice*. Boston: Northeastern University Press, 1996, p. 41.

9. William L. Shirer, *The Rise and Fall of the Third Reich*. New York: Fawcett Crest Books, 1962, p. 580.

Chapter 2: Unthinkable Things

10. Quoted in Pick, *Simon Wiesenthal*, p. 54.

11. Lingens. "Who Is Simon Wiesenthal?" p. 7.

12. Quoted in Levy, *The Wiesenthal File*, p. 38.

13. Levy, *The Wiesenthal File*, p. 39.

14. Pick, *Simon Wiesenthal*, p. 57.

15. Quoted in Pick, *Simon Wiesenthal*, p. 58.

16. Quoted in Pick, *Simon Wiesenthal*, pp. 31–32.

17. Levy, *The Wiesenthal File*, p. 48.

18. Quoted in Levy, *The Wiesenthal File*, p. 48.

19. Quoted in Levy, *The Wiesenthal File*, p. 53.

20. Levy, *The Wiesenthal File*, p. 56.

21. Quoted in Levy, *The Wiesenthal File*, p 61.

22. Quoted in Levy, *The Wiesenthal File*, p. 48.

23. Quoted in Levy, *The Wiesenthal File*, p. 43.

24. Quoted in Levy, *The Wiesenthal File*, p 43.

Chapter 3: A World We Never Made

25. Wiesenthal, *Justice Not Vengeance*, p. 29.

26. Quoted in Pick, *Simon Wiesenthal*, p. 83.

27. Wiesenthal, *Justice Not Vengeance*, p. 32.

28. Wiesenthal, *Justice Not Vengeance*, p. 32.

29. Pick, *Simon Wiesenthal*, p. 86.

30. Wiesenthal, *Justice Not Vengeance*, p. 33.

31. Levy, *The Wiesenthal File*, p. 71.

32. Eleanor Shapiro, "Eichmann Drama Covers Escape, Capture, Execution," *Northern California Jewish Bulletin*, April 8, 1994, pp. PG.

33. Quoted in Wiesenthal, *Justice Not Vengeance*, p. 67.

34. Wiesenthal, *Justice Not Vengeance*, p. 67.

35. Wiesenthal, *Justice Not Vengeance*, p. 67.

36. Quoted in Levy, *The Wiesenthal File*, p. 75.

37. Quoted in *Response: The Wiesenthal Center World Report*, vol. 20, no. 1, Winter/Spring 1999, cover.

38. Simon Wiesenthal, *The Sunflower: On the Possibilities and Limits of Forgiveness*. Revised and expanded edition. New York: Schocken Books, 1997, pp. 94–95.

39. Quoted in Levy, *The Wiesenthal File*, p. 78.

40. Quoted in Levy, *The Wiesenthal File*, p. 79.

41. Levy, *The Wiesenthal File*, p. 80.

42. Quoted in Levy, *The Wiesenthal File*, p. 82.

43. Quoted in Levy, *The Wiesenthal File*, p. 82.

Chapter 4: Occupation: Nazi Hunter

44. Quoted in Wiesenthal, *Justice Not Vengeance,* p. 36.

45. Wiesenthal, *Justice Not Vengeance,* p. 36.

46. Wiesenthal, *Justice Not Vengeance,* p. 37.

47. Quoted in Levy, *The Wiesenthal File*, p. 85.

48. Quoted in Levy, *The Wiesenthal File*, p. 84.

49. *Cleveland Jewish News*, "The Trial of Adolf Eichmann," May 2, 1997, pp. PG.

50. Wiesenthal, *Justice Not Vengeance,* p. 69.

51. Wiesenthal, *Justice Not Vengeance,* p. 69.

52. Wiesenthal, *Justice Not Vengeance,* p. 70.

53. Wiesenthal, *Justice Not Vengeance,* p. 104.

Chapter 5: In the Shadow of the Holocaust

54. Pick, *Simon Wiesenthal*, p. 139.

55. Quoted in Levy, *The Wiesenthal File*, p. 17.

56. Levy, *The Wiesenthal File*, p. 17.

57. Pick, *Simon Wiesenthal*, p. 177.

58. Pick, *Simon Wiesenthal*, p. 179.

59. Yehund Bauer, quoted in James M. Glass. *"Life Unworthy of Life": Racial Phobia and Mass Murder in Hitler's Germany.* New York: Basic Books, 1997, p. 5.

60. Wiesenthal, *Justice Not Vengeance,* p. 84.

61. Quoted in Pick, *Simon Wiesenthal*, p. 185.

62. Quoted in Levy, *The Wiesenthal File*, p. 239.

63. Quoted in Levy, *The Wiesenthal File*, p. 239.

64. Quoted in Pick, *Simon Wiesenthal*, p. 192.

65. Quoted in Wiesenthal, *Justice Not Vengeance,* p. 140.

66. Wiesenthal, *Justice Not Vengeance,* p. 151.

Chapter 6: To the Ends of the Earth

67. Quoted in Pick, *Simon Wiesenthal*, p. 219.

68. Wiesenthal, *Justice Not Vengeance,* p. 89.

69. Wiesenthal, *Justice Not Vengeance,* p. 93.

70. Wiesenthal, *Justice Not Vengeance,* p. 93.

71. Wiesenthal, *Justice Not Vengeance,* p. 93.

72. Quoted in Levy, *The Wiesenthal File*, p. 339.

73. Quoted in Levy, *The Wiesenthal File*, p. 346.

74. Quoted in Levy, *The Wiesenthal File*, p. 343.

75. Levy, *The Wiesenthal File*, p. 347.

76. Quoted in Pick, *Simon Wiesenthal*, p. 271.

77. *Response: The Wiesenthal Center World Report*, vol. 19, no. 3, Fall 1998, p. 3.

78. Eli M. Rosenbaum with William Hoffer, *Betrayal: The Untold Story of the Kurt Waldheim Investigation and Cover-Up.* New York: St. Martin's Press, 1993, p. 36.

79. Quoted in Levy, *The Wiesenthal File*, p. 413.

80. Rosenbaum, *Betrayal*, p. 355.

Chapter 7: In the Eye of the Storm

81. Quoted in Levy, *The Wiesenthal File*, p. 194.

82. Patricia Blake reported by Ann Blackman/Moscow, World, "At Last, a Tomorrow Without Battle: Andrei Sakharov: 1921–1989," *Time*, December 25, 1989, p. 23.

83. Wiesenthal, *Justice Not Vengeance,* p. 198.

84. Wiesenthal, *Justice Not Vengeance,* p. 200.

85. Quoted in Blake, "At Last, a Tomorrow Without Battle," p. 25.

86. Isabel Fonseca, *Bury Me Standing: The Gypsies and Their Journey.* New York: Random House, 1995, p. 253.

87. Quoted in Fonseca, *Bury Me Standing*, p. 261.

88. Pick, *Simon Wiesenthal*, p. 242.

89. Pick, *Simon Wiesenthal*, p. 119.

90. Quoted in Jochen von Lang, *The Secretary—Martin Bormann: The Man Who Manipulated Hitler.* New York: Random House, 1979, pp. 355, 356.

91. Quoted in Levy, *The Wiesenthal File*, p. 137.

92. Rosenbaum, *Betrayal*, p. 312.

93. Quoted in Pick, *Simon Wiesenthal*, p. 231.

94. Quoted in Pick, *Simon Wiesenthal*, p. 232.

95. Wiesenthal, *Justice Not Vengeance,* p. vii.

For Further Reading

Books

Anne Frank, *The Diary of a Young Girl: The Definitive Edition.* Ed. Otto H. Frank and Mirjam Pressler. New York: Bantam Books, 1997. Anne Frank's father restored material that was deleted in the first publication of the famous diary. The book has been widely read by young people.

Laura S. Jeffrey, *Simon Wiesenthal: Tracking Down Nazi Criminals.* Springfield, NJ: Enslow Publishers, 1997. This biography for young people includes information on his later years.

Iris Noble, *Nazi Hunter: Simon Wiesenthal.* New York: J. Messner, 1979. This biography for young people discusses Wiesenthal's early life and experiences in the camps.

Simon Wiesenthal, *The Sunflower: On the Possibilities and Limits of Forgiveness.* Revised and expanded edition. New York: Schocken Books, 1997. Wiesenthal's account of his meeting with a dying Nazi soldier is regarded as one of his best books. This volume includes a symposium in which prominent people discuss their own attitudes toward forgiveness.

Websites

Facing History and Ourselves

(http://info_boston@facing.org/). The site offers information on Holocaust studies, along with school programs for increasing tolerance and combating anti-Semitism.

Liberators' testimonies

(htttp://remember.org/witness/liberators. html). This site contains descriptions of the camps from the soldiers who liberated them.

Response

(www.wiesenthal.com/response/v19n3 worldreport.html). The text of the Simon Wiesenthal Center magazine features much of the same material as the print version.

Simon Wiesenthal biography

(www.wiesenthal.com/swies/index.html). This Wiesenthal Center site offers a brief overview of Wiesenthal's life and work.

Simon Wiesenthal Center

(www.wiesenthal.org:80/). This is the main page of the Los Angeles study center and Museum.

Simon Wiesenthal photos

(www.wiesenthal.com/swies/wiesphot. htm). The staff of the Wiesenthal Center has created an online display of Wiesenthal photos.

United States Holocaust Memorial Museum

(www.ushmm.org/). The Museum's home page includes links to online exhibits and other Holocaust information.

Works Consulted

Books

Isabel Fonseca, *Bury Me Standing: The Gypsies and Their Journey*. New York: Random House, 1995. Fonseca spent several months living with the Gypsies and studying their ways. The result is a readable account, filled with human-interest stories.

Viktor E. Frankl, *Man's Search for Meaning*. Boston: Beacon Press, 1959. Paperback ed. New York: Washington Square Press, 1985. An Auschwitz survivor's account of his experiences and their effect on his development of Logotherapy, a new approach to psychiatry.

James M. Glass, *"Life Unworthy of Life": Racial Phobia and Mass Murder in Hitler's Germany*. New York: Basic Books, 1997. This study of Nazi euthanasia captures the horror of this murderous program.

Adolf Hitler, *Mein Kampf*. Trans. by Ralph Manheim. Boston: Houghton Mifflin, 1971. In this lengthy work, Adolf Hitler told the story of his life and the beginnings of his political philosophy.

Ernest Klee, Wili Dressen, and Volker Riess, eds. Trans. Deborah Burnstone, *"The Good Old Days": The Holocaust As Seen by Its Perpetrators and Bystanders*. New York: Konecky & Konecky, 1991. This chilling account of the Einsatzgruppen killing squads uses testimonies from the killers themselves to tell the story.

John Laffin, *Hitler Warned Us*. London: Brassey's, 1995. Military historian Laffin examines the rise of Adolf Hitler and his Third Reich.

Jochen von Lang, *The Secretary—Martin Bormann: The Man Who Manipulated Hitler*. New York: Random House, 1979. A biography that looks deep into the life and character of the man who became Hitler's confidant and secretary.

Alan Levy, *The Wiesenthal File*. Grand Rapids, MI: William B. Eerdmans Publishing, 1993. Levy looks at some of Wiesenthal's most significant cases, and brings them to life in a book that reads like a thriller.

Robert Jay Lifton, *The Nazi Doctors: Medical Killing and the Psychology of Genocide*. New York: Basic Books, 1986. An American doctor investigates the activities of doctors in the Nazi killing machine.

Kevin Mahoney, ed., *In Pursuit of Justice: Examining the Evidence of the Holocaust*. Washington, DC: United States Holocaust Memorial Council, n.d. The Holocaust Museum's overview of the Nuremberg Trials gives excerpts from actual testimony and descriptions of the various crimes committed by the Reich.

Joachim Neugroschel, ed., *The Shtetl: A Creative Anthology of Jewish Life in Eastern Europe*. New York: Richard Marek Publishers, 1979. A literary anthology of the life and lore of Eastern European Jews.

Hella Pick, *Simon Wiesenthal: A Life in Search of Justice*. Boston: Northeastern University Press. 1996. Pick's biography strikes a nice balance between Wiesenthal the man and Wiesenthal the Nazi Hunter.

Eli M. Rosenbaum with William Hoffer, *Betrayal: The Untold Story of the Kurt Waldheim Investigation and Cover-Up.* New York: St. Martin's Press, 1993. Rosenbaum analyzes the Waldheim investigation from beginning to end.

William L. Shirer, *The Rise and Fall of the Third Reich.* New York: Fawcett Crest Books, 1962. Shirer's classic history covers Nazism from its beginnings in the 1920s to the end of World War II.

Margot Stern Strom and William S. Parsons, *Facing History and Ourselves: Holocaust and Human Behavior.* Watertown, MA: Intentional Educations, Inc., 1982. A resource book that draws on many sources to describe anti-Semitism and the Holocaust.

Elie Wiesel, *Night.* New York: Hill & Wang, 1960; New York: Bantam Books, 1982. Wiesel's powerful account of his experiences in Auschwitz is considered a classic of Holocaust literature.

Simon Wiesenthal, *Justice Not Vengeance.* New York: Grove Weidenfeld, 1989. Wiesenthal wrote this second autobiography in his eightieth year.

————,*K2 Mauthausen.* Linz, Austria: Ibis Verlag, 1946. Wiesenthal's first published book features a selection of the drawings he made at Mauthausen.

————, *Ich Jagte Eichmann* ("I Hunted Eichmann"). Gütersloh, Germany: Bertelsman, 1961. Wiesenthal's account of his involvement in the long hunt for the architect of the Final Solution.

Periodicals

Patricia Blake, reported by Ann Blackman/Moscow, World, "At Last, a Tomorrow Without Battle: Andrei Sakharov: 1921–1989," *Time,* December 25, 1989.

Jordan Bofante, "War Crimes: Where Have All the Nazis Gone?" *Time,* August 9, 1993.

Cleveland Jewish News, "The Trial of Adolf Eichmann," May 2, 1997.

St. Louis Post-Dispatch, "Eyewitness to the Holocaust: 50 Years Ago, Joseph Pulitzer II Helped Bring Home to America the Full Horror of Atrocities in Nazi Germany's Death Camps," April 30, 1995.

Sue Fishkoff, "The Righteous Among Us," *Jerusalem Post,* September 13, 1996.

Richard Hecht, "The Face of Modern Anti-Semitism," *The Center Magazine,* March–April 1981.

Stephen Lutz, "People Must Acknowledge Their Tendencies to Do Evil," *University Wire,* September 29, 1997.

Response: The Wiesenthal Center World Report, vol. 19, no. 3, Fall 1998.

Response: The Wiesenthal Center World Report, vol. 20, no. 1, Winter/Spring 1999.

A. James Rudin, "Since 1945, Nazi Hunter Wiesenthal Has Never Forgotten He's a 'Survivor,'" *Sacramento Bee,* January 16, 1999.

Gitta Sereny, "Colloquy with A Conscience," *The Daily Telegraph,* October 8, 1971.

Eleanor Shapiro, "Eichmann Drama Covers Escape, Capture, Execution," *Northern California Jewish Bulletin,* April 8, 1994.

Internet Sites and CD-ROMs

Colliers Encyclopedia CD-ROM, online at www.elibrary.com

Jan Larsson, *Sweden:* "Swedish Portraits. Raoul Wallenberg." *Countries of the World* CD-ROM. Parsippany, NJ: Bureau Development Inc., 1991.

Faith Nguyen, "With Liberty and Justice for All: The Skokie Right to March Case," University of Virginia, n.d. www.people.virginia.edu/~fen5y/skokie4web.html.

ThinkQuest Team, *Jewish Ghettos.* http://library.advanced.org/12307/index.html. 1997.

Index

Wiesenthal, Asher (father), 13, 14–15
Wiesenthal, Cyla
  as Irena Kowalska, 27, 29
  in Janowskà labor camp, 24–25
  Nazi hunting and, 44, 65
  in railway repair works, 25–26
  reunion of Simon Wiesenthal and, 43–44
  supposed death of, 35–36
Wiesenthal, Hillel (brother), 13, 18
Wiesenthal, Paulinka (daughter), 44, 94
Wiesenthal, Rosa (mother)
  death of, 24, 27
  remarriage of, 18
  under Soviet Union, 21
  during Wiesenthal's childhood, 13, 15–16
Wiesenthal, Simon
  characteristics of, 74, 93, 95, 96
  on charges that he wanted publicity, 95
  childhood of, 13–17
  collective guilt and, 32, 78
  education of, 17–19
  Gypsies and, 91–92, 93
  on his appearance upon liberation, 39
  on importance of being witness, 11, 12

is saved from death by
  Bodnar, 23
  Kohlrautz, 29, 31
  partisans, 32–33
  Staniszewski, 36
in Janowskà labor camp, 24–25
on Jewish collaborators, 52
on Jews in Buczacz, 13, 16
justice and
  belief in, 14
Nazi hunting and, 12
Kreisky and, 79
on Lvov ghetto, 24
marriage of, 19
as Nazi hunter
  of Bormann, 58–59, 93
  of Braunsteiner, 67, 71–73
  with Documentation Center, 67
  of Eichmann, 56–58, 63, 93
  with Jewish Historical Documentation Center (Linz), 46–48, 60
  of Mengele, 67, 71
  reasons for, 12, 44, 48, 59
  of Roschmann, 74, 75
  rules for, 52, 71, 73, 78
  of Silberbauer, 61–63
  of Stangl, 67–70
  threats against family

and, 65–67
  of Wagner, 75–77
  with War Crimes Office, 39–40, 42, 45–46
with Organization for Rehabilitation and Training (ORT), 61
in railway repair works, 25–26
on roundup of his mother, 27
Sakharov and, 89–90
suicide attempts of, 34
Wallenberg and, 87–88
on Waltke, 34
Wiesel and, 92–93
works of
  I Hunted Eichmann, 63
  Justice Not Vengeance, 12, 95
  KZ Mauthausen, 36
  Murderers Among Us, The, 93, 95
  Sunflower, The, 37–38, 44–45, 95–96
Wiesenthal's Law, 52, 78
World Jewish Congress (WJC), 60, 82, 83, 84, 85
World War I, 14–15, 16
World War II, 21

Yad Vashem, 60–61
Yugoslavia, 83

Zimet (Zimmet), David, 52

Picture Credits

Cover photo: © 1999 Erich Lessing/Magnum Photos, Inc.
Archive Photos, 47, 59, 67, 68, 70, 75, 77, 83, 89
Archive Photos/Bernard Gotfryd, 84
Archive Photos/Anthony Potter Collection, 20
Bundesarchive Koblenz/Courtesy of the Simon Wiesenthal Center
 Beit HaShoah Museum of Tolerance Library/Archives, Los An-
 geles, CA, 24, 30
Corbis, 37, 41, 57, 65, 87
Corbis/Bettmann, 14, 95
Corbis/Hulton-Deutsch Collection, 42
Anne Frank Fonds, Basel/Anne Frank House, Amsterdam/
 Archive Photos, 61
Main Commission for the Investigation of Nazi War Crimes, cour-
 tesy of USHMM Photo Archives, 56
National Archives, 10, 21, 25, 27, 28, 31, 33, 35, 50, 53, 54
Simon Wiesenthal Center, 12, 17, 19, 45, 52, 60, 64, 73, 80, 91, 96

About the Author

Linda Jacobs Altman has written many books for children and young people, including *Amelia's Road*, the story of a young migrant farmworker, and *Genocide: The Systematic Killing of a People*. She has also written many books on Jewish topics for young people, including *Life on an Israeli Kibbutz* (Lucent) and *Forever Outsiders: Jews and History From Ancient Times to August 1935* (Blackbirch).

She lives with her husband, Richard, and an assortment of four-legged friends in Clearlake, California. When not writing she enjoys studying Spanish and collecting VHS movies.